To be a Five Talent Servant

Jason Groube

To Be a Five Talent Servant
Published by Jason Groube
with Castle Publishing Ltd
New Zealand

© 2022 Jason Groube
jason.selinagroube@outlook.com

ISBN 978-0-473-61156-9 (Softcover)
ISBN 978-0-473-61157-6 (ePUB)
ISBN 978-0-473-61158-3 (Kindle)

Editing:
Geoff Vause

Production & Typesetting:
Andrew Killick
Castle Publishing Services
www.castlepublishing.co.nz

Cover Design:
Paul Smith

All Scripture quotations, unless otherwise indicated,
are taken from the Holy Bible, New International Version®, NIV®.
Copyright ©1973, 1978, 1984, 2011 by Biblica, Inc.™
Used by permission of Zondervan. All rights reserved worldwide.
www.zondervan.com

Scripture quotations marked (KJV) are taken from
The Authorised (King James) Version.
Reproduced by permission of the Crown's patentee,
Cambridge University Press.

ALL RIGHTS RESERVED

No part of this publication may be reproduced,
stored in a retrieval system, or transmitted
in any form or by any means, electronic, mechanical,
photocopying, recording or otherwise,
without prior written permission from the author.

To be a Five Talent Servant

Contents

Introduction	9
Part One: Truths Within this Parable	**15**
An End Days Parable	17
The Lord Jesus Christ	19
The Holy Spirit	23
Mankind	29
The Works Required	33
The Significance of the Talents and Minas	37
The Hard Task Master	43
Part Two: The One Talent Servant	**47**
Introducing the One Talent Servant	49
Refusing to Submit	51
Burying the Truth	55
Bearing Fruit	61
Part Three: The Two Talent Servant	**65**
Introducing the Two Talent Servant	67
Who are Two Talent Servants?	71
Our Gracious God	73
Self-Righteousness Versus God's Righteousness	75

A Duel/Dual to the Death	85
Our Identity Struggle	101
Mediocrity	107
A Milk Diet	111
Eyes on Man	115
Moving On	121
Part Four: The Five Talent Servant	**123**
Introducing the Five Talent Servant	125
Who are Five Talent Servants?	129
True Repentance	133
United in Christ	137
United in His Suffering	143
United in His Word	147
United in Obedience	151
Biblical Examples	155
Conclusion	167

The Parable of the Talents

For the kingdom of heaven is as a man travelling into a far country, who called his own servants, and delivered unto them his goods.

And unto one he gave five talents, to another two, and to another one; to every man according to his several ability; and straightway took his journey.

He that had received the five talents went and traded with the same, and made them another five talents. And likewise he that had received two, he also gained another two. But he that had received one went and digged in the earth, and hid his lord's money.

After a long time the lord of those servants cometh, and reckoneth with them. And he that had received five talents came and brought another five talents, saying, Lord, thou deliveredst unto me five talents: behold, I have gained beside them five talents more.

His lord said unto him, Well done, thou good and faithful servant: thou hast been faithful over a few things, I will make thee ruler over many things: enter thou into the joy of thy lord.

He also that had received two talents came and said, Lord thou deliveredst unto me two talents: behold, I have gained two other talents beside them. His lord said unto him, Well done, good and faithful servant, thou hast been faithful over a few things, I will make thee ruler over many things: enter thou into the joy of the lord.

He who had received the one talent came and said, Lord, I knew thee that thou art a hard man, reaping where thou hast not sown, and gathering where thou hast not strawed: And I was afraid, and went and hid thy talent in the earth: lo, there thou hast that is thine.

His lord answered and said unto him, Thou wicked and slothful servant, thou knewest that I reap where I sowed not, and gather where I have not strawed: Thou oughtest therefore to have put my money to the exchangers (*bankers*), and at my coming I should have received mine own with usury (*interest*).

Take therefore the talent from him, and give it unto him which hath ten talents.

For unto every one that hath shall be given, and he shall have abundance: but from him that hath not shall be taken away even that which he hath.

And cast ye the unprofitable servant into outer darkness: there shall be weeping and gnashing of teeth.

Matthew 25:14-30 (KJV)

Introduction

In 1997 God showed me an interpretation of the talent parable completely different to all the versions I had previously heard. Over 20 years later, I'm more convinced what I saw unfold is Biblically sound, and the Holy Spirit revealed it.

It sounds dangerous and red flags are probably appearing – fair enough for the spiritually minded and critical thinker. I'm confident this interpretation isn't from me, but from the Lord.

In 1997 I asked and prayed God would give His interpretation of this parable. I was not completely convinced the way this particular parable was interpreted was correct.

At this stage of my life, God was also showing me His way of thinking and the standard interpretation of this parable didn't seem to fit.

What I believe Christ revealed to me was consistent with His Word and His priorities. Everything within this parable is there for a reason, and it's consistent with God's way. It has been more than 20 years for me to decide what I believed was wrong, but the opposite has happened.

The interpretation has only strengthened and it fits more snugly into God's hand, and is consistent with Christ's truths and principles.

I also realised I would be stepping on many toes and I needed to be absolutely sure before I wrote this book.

If it's something God has shown me, I must be obedient to what He has called me to do, despite the consequences.

This parable is consistent with many truths and principles throughout Scripture. It points us to Christ and not ourselves. It relies on the work of the Holy Spirit and not man, yet it still gives us the freedom of choice.

It makes us accountable to what God has offered us.

> It is written: 'As surely as I live,' says the Lord, 'every knee will bow before me; every tongue will acknowledge God.' Each of us will give an account of ourselves to God. (Romans 14:11)

This parable carries much weight, and gives us much hope. It doesn't discriminate against anyone who truly seeks the Lord, it promises all can be 'Five Talent Servants'.

The Standard Interpretation

The most common interpretation of this parable is about talents and abilities God has given us. Are we using these talents and abilities to serve the Lord? It doesn't matter if you feel you only have one talent to offer, as long as you're being faithful with that one talent.

There have been other interpretations of this parable, but this is the most prevalent. It sounds good, because we have been given the opportunity to use our gifts, and if we don't, we're denying God the natural abilities He has given us.

It's understandable this version has never really been challenged, because it gives us meaning. It promises we all have a useful purpose in God's kingdom through what we offer. Through our talents and abilities, we can make a difference.

When I started to see it in a different light, the standard interpretation of this parable started to fall apart.

Name one Christian around you today, who is a 'Five Talent Servant'? This includes yourself. And if you think you know others who are, ask them if they think they are?

But the most telling question is, would you ever consider yourself to be a 'Five Talent Servant'?

The minute we think we're a 'Five Talent Servant', we're convicted of pride. We love to say of ourselves we're 'One Talent Servants'. Anything higher than this would be elevating ourselves. We usually identify ourselves with the 'One Talent Servant' or if we're brave, the 'Two Talent Servant', rather than the 'Five Talent Servant'.

If you follow the logic, only those who are oozing with talents and abilities can fit this description of the 'Five Talent Servant'.

And we, being humble Christians, will only consider ourselves 'One' or even maybe, 'Two Talent Servants'.

We align ourselves with the servant who got thrown into hell, or the servant who accomplished not much and received no additional blessing.

> Take therefore the talent from him, and give it unto him who hath ten talents. For unto every one that hath shall be given, and he shall have abundance: but from him that hath not shall be taken away even that which he hath. (Matthew 25:28-29)

It's hard to find anyone who might fit the 'Five Talent Servant' concerning natural gifts. Even the great men and women of the Bible don't fit this.

For example, the Apostle Paul. If you try and put him in this category, it doesn't work.

> If I must boast, I will boast of the things showing my weakness. (2 Corinthians 11:30)

> But whatever were gains to me I now consider loss for the sake of Christ. What is more, I consider everything a loss because

of the surpassing worth of knowing Christ Jesus my Lord, for whose sake I have lost all things. I consider them garbage that I may gain Christ. (Philippians 3:7-8)

Paul never relied on his talents and abilities to further the kingdom of God, he relied on what Christ did on the cross.

For Christ did not send me to baptise, but to preach the gospel – not with wisdom or eloquence, lest the cross of Christ be emptied of its power.
  For the message of the cross is foolishness to those who are perishing, but to us who are being saved it is the power of God. (1 Corinthians 1:17-18)

Paul was willing to become a fool in the eyes of this world, so he may gain Christ.

There is another problem operating in our natural gifts. You may be a preacher, sportsman, evangelist, servant, teacher, musician, intellectual, entrepreneur, jack of all trades and much more, but whatever we find ourselves naturally good at, this will be our gifts.

Here is the problem…

When we operate in what we're naturally good at, or become familiar with, we have the ability to go it alone, without dependence on God. The nature within us is fiercely independent of God and we will drift in this direction if we're not keeping this in check.

You'll find many Christians who have served the Lord for years, dissatisfied, or feeling empty. They've gone from what may have started spiritually and allowed their natural self to take over, without realising the authority and power of Christ is diminishing.

When we're operating in what we're naturally good at, we have the tendency to fall into the trap of relying on our own ability. The

Bible says this trap is nearly impossible to avoid unless we obey what Christ said.

> He said to them all: 'Whoever wants to be my disciple must deny themselves and take up their cross daily and follow me.' (Luke 9:23)

You may start to understand why I wasn't completely at peace with this interpretation of this Talent Parable.

I'm not suggesting we stop operating in what we're gifted at. If God has led you to use your talents and abilities, you have to be faithful and obedient to His will.

If He chooses, God has and will continue to use us in what we're naturally good at.

Talents and abilities can be used for the kingdom of God, but this parable isn't talking about our natural gifts.

It's talking about the ability of God, Christ Jesus, and the Holy Spirit and what part we play in this.

This parable and a similar parable found in Luke 19:11-26 have truths illuminating this.

PART I
Truths Within this Parable

Chapter 1

An End Days Parable

Before we look into this parable, we must understand this is an 'end days' parable. Jesus was speaking about the end times and this was one of the parables He used.

> As Jesus was sitting on the Mount of Olives, the disciples came to him privately. 'Tell us,' they said, 'when will this happen and what will be the sign of your coming and of the end of the age?' (Matthew 24:3)

For the next two chapters Jesus talks about things concerning the end times, but for one exception. Jesus prophesies the destruction of the Temple in 70 AD. Everything else was end days.

He talks about guarding against deception, false messiahs, false prophets, many turning away from the faith, others standing firm, the end being like the days of Noah, distress never to be equalled, cutting this time short for the sake of the elect, the Son of Man returning with power and great glory, angels with loud trumpets, the gathering of the elect and other end time matters.

Jesus warns us to be ready:

> So you also must be ready, because the Son of Man will come at an hour when you do not expect him. (Matthew 24:44)

To emphasise this, He uses examples and parables. The example is the faithful and wise servant (Matthew 24:45-47), and the wicked servant (Matthew 24:48-51). Two parables; the parable of the ten virgins (Matthew 25:1-12), and the parable of the talents (Matthew 25:14-30).

These parables warn us about the condition we may find ourselves in, upon His return. The parable of the talents is about us being ready to give an account of what He has given us.

> It is written: 'As surely as I live,' says the Lord, 'every knee will bow before me; every tongue will acknowledge God.' (Romans 14:11-12)

Each of us will give an account of ourselves to God. When Jesus returns, what condition will He find us in?

Chapter 2

The Lord Jesus Christ

The lord or master within this parable represents Jesus Christ.

Christ is talking about the end times. The lord going away to a far country and returning is about Jesus leaving this earth and one day, returning.

> After he said this, he was taken up before their very eyes, and a cloud hid him from their sight. They were looking intently up into the sky as he was going, when suddenly two men dressed in white stood beside them.
> 'Men of Galilee,' they said, 'why do you stand here looking into the sky? This same Jesus, who has been taken from you into heaven, will come back in the same way you have seen him go into heaven.' (Acts 1:9-11)

Jesus will return despite the mockers.

> For, 'In a little while, he who is coming will come and will not delay.' (Hebrews 10:37)

> Above all, you must understand in the last days scoffers will come, scoffing and following their own evil desires.
> They will say, 'Where is this "coming" he promised? Ever

since our ancestors died, everything goes on as it has since the beginning of creation.' (2 Peter 3:3-4)

God requires us to live a holy and righteous life.

> For the grace of God has appeared offering salvation to all people.
> It teaches us to say 'No' to ungodliness and worldly passions, and to live self-controlled, upright and godly lives in this present age, while we wait for the blessed hope – the appearing of the glory of our great God and Saviour, Jesus Christ... (Titus 2:11-13)

> 'And now, dear children, continue in him, so when he appears we may be confident and unashamed before him at his coming.' (1 John 2:28)

When Jesus returns, our motives and deep desires will be exposed.

> Therefore judge nothing before the appointed time; wait until the Lord comes.
> He will bring to light what is hidden in darkness and will expose the motives of the heart. Each will receive their praise from God. (1 Corinthians 4:5)

Jesus will return and reward all who have been faithful to Him.

> Look, I am coming soon! My reward is with me, and I will give to each person according to what they have done.
> I am the Alpha and the Omega, the First and the Last, the Beginning and the End. (Revelation 22:12-13)

Jesus didn't leave us alone when He returned to His Heavenly Father. He left us the Holy Spirit.

Chapter 3

The Holy Spirit

I need to be absolutely correct with this next truth, because if I'm not, it could be blasphemy.

The talents or money given by the master represents the Holy Spirit. I need to be certain what I'm saying is correct. There are examples within the parable proving this.

> But very truly I tell you, it is for your good that I'm going away. Unless I go away, the Advocate will not come to you; but if I go, I will send him to you. (John 16:7)

The master in the parable only gives the money when he goes away. This doesn't apply to our natural abilities, because we were born with these.

The parable says the money was given to his servants when he departed, not when they were born. And Jesus says, unless He goes away, the Holy Spirit can't come.

The money within this parable can only be used for the master's work. The servant with the one talent couldn't use it for anything else.

> And I was afraid, and went and hid thy talent in the earth: lo, there thou hast that is thine. (Matthew 25:25 KJV)

Why didn't this wicked servant run away with it and use it for his own selfish gain? Because the money in this parable represents the Holy Spirit. And the Holy Spirit can't be manipulated by man for his own selfish purpose.

> But when he, the Spirit of Truth, comes, he will guide you into all the truth. He will not speak on his own; he will speak only what he hears, and he will tell you what is yet to come.
> He will glorify me because it is from me that he will receive what he will make known to you. All that belongs to the Father is mine.
> That is why I said the Spirit will receive from me what he will make known to you. (John 16:13-15)

The money could only be used for the master's purpose and nothing else. We can easily use our natural abilities for our own gain without acknowledging God for them. The parable specifically says the money couldn't be used for anything but the master's purpose.

Only the Holy Spirit has the ability to accomplish Christ's will, uncompromised. The will of Christ can't be accomplished without the Holy Spirit, and mankind can't manipulate the Holy Spirit for their own gain.

These talents, or sums of money, carry great significance. There is an accountability attached to them. The master requires results or gains and if no gain is accomplished, dire consequences follow.

Disobedience holds nothing less than hell.

> "And cast ye the unprofitable servant into the outer darkness: there shall be weeping and gnashing of teeth." (Matthew 25:30 KJV)

Whenever this statement is used, it always refers to hell.

> The Son of Man will send out his angels, and they will weed out of his kingdom everything causing sin and all who do evil. They will throw them into the blazing furnace, where there will be weeping and gnashing of teeth. (Matthew 13:41-42)

> Once again, the kingdom of heaven is like a net that was let down into the lake and caught all kinds of fish. When it was full, the fishermen pulled it up on the shore. They sat down and collected the good fish in baskets, but threw the bad away.
> This is how it will be at the end of the age. The angels will come and separate the wicked from the righteous and throw them into the blazing furnace, where there will be weeping and gnashing of teeth. (Matthew 13:47-50)

The significance of the Talents is important to God. His wrath isn't kindled against us because of our laziness, but because we reject His Messenger, the Holy Spirit.

The Spirit convicts the world of sin. The sin the Spirit convicts the world of is the rejection of the Lord Jesus Christ.

> When he (Holy Spirit) comes, he will prove the world to be in the wrong about sin and righteousness and judgment: about sin, because people do not believe in me (Jesus Christ). (John 16:8-9)

> It is God who makes both us and you stand firm in Christ. He anointed us, set his seal of ownership on us, and put his Spirit in our hearts as a deposit, guaranteeing what is to come. (2 Corinthians 1:21-22)

Now, what about the different talents given. Does it mean the Holy Spirit is unequally given?

No, and yes.

There is a similar parable where the master gives his servants money to carry out his work. It's also an end time's parable.

> While they were listening to this, he went on to tell them a parable, because he was near Jerusalem and the people thought the kingdom of God was going to appear at once.
>
> He said: 'A man of noble birth went to a distant country to have himself appointed king and to return. He called ten of his servants and gave them ten minas. "Put this money to work," he said, "until I come back."' (Luke 19:11-14)

Here we see the money is distributed evenly. The Holy Spirit is the One who reveals the righteousness of God to mankind. The opportunity is equally given because God has revealed Himself throughout the earth (John 16:8).

> For in the gospel the righteousness of God is revealed – a righteousness that is by faith from first to last, as it is written: 'The righteous will live by faith.'
>
> The wrath of God is being revealed from heaven against all the godlessness and wickedness of people, who suppress the truth by their wickedness, since what may be known about God is plain to them, because God has made it plain to them.
>
> For since the creation of the world God's invisible qualities – his eternal power and divine nature – have been clearly seen, being understood from what has been made, so people are without excuse. (Romans 1:17-20)

People have no excuse, because whether they have heard the

gospel of Christ or not, the wickedness of men and women has rejected the righteousness of God.

Wherever Christianity is preached, there is now the righteousness of Christ Jesus that is rejected by men and women. It's the Holy Spirit who goes throughout the world revealing the Truth.

To deal with the issue of the different talents given and ask whether there are differing measures of the Holy Spirit, we need to look at the wording within the parable.

> And unto one he gave five talents, to another two, and to another one; to every man according to his several ability; and straightway took his journey. (Matthew 25:15 KJV)

The NIV says, '…each according to his ability'.

The Bible makes it clear, the more we're obedient to Christ, the deeper our relationship becomes. The revelation of our Heavenly Father and Jesus Christ increases and this is made possible through the Holy Spirit.

The more obedient we're to Christ, the more of the Holy Spirit is imparted to us. The master gave different measures of talents because of their abilities. We're given more of the Holy Spirit because of our obedience.

It's the Holy Spirit getting us to accomplish the will of God. Whatever we accomplish here on earth, must be done through the Holy Spirit. Without the Holy Spirit, we can accomplish nothing.

The talents made it possible for the servants to accomplish the master's work, and the Holy Spirit makes it possible to accomplish the works of Christ Jesus.

CHAPTER 4

Mankind

The servants within this parable represent mankind.

One of the teachings of this parable is Christ is referring to only Christians, because He uses the term, 'servants.' Generally, servants of God are only Christians, but not in this parable in Matthew 25:14-30, or the parable in Luke 19:11-26.

Servants are accountable to their masters and those who are not servants, are not accountable to the master. The point is: all of mankind are servants, because we will all be accountable to God.

> Turn to me and be saved, all you ends of the earth; for I am God, and there is no other. By myself I have sworn, my mouth has uttered in all integrity a word that will not be revoked: Before me every knee will bow; by me every tongue will swear. (Isaiah 45:22-23)

This verse is confirmed in Romans 14:11-12,

> It is written: 'As surely as I live,' says the Lord, 'every knee will bow before me; every tongue will acknowledge God.' Each of us will give an account of ourselves to God.

> For since the creation of the world God's invisible qualities – his

eternal power and divine nature – have been clearly seen, being understood from what has been made, so people are without excuse. (Romans 1:20)

The sole reason mankind is here on this earth is to come into fellowship with the kingdom of God.

> The Son is the image of the invisible God, the firstborn over all creation. For in him all things were created: things in heaven and on earth, visible and invisible, whether thrones or powers or rulers or authorities; all things have been created through him and for him. (Colossians 1:15-16)

We clearly see, we were created for Christ. We are automatically accountable to Him.

The Bible says we will all be accountable.

> Therefore God exalted him to the highest place and gave him the name that is above every name, that at the name of Jesus every knee should bow, in heaven and on earth and under the earth, and every tongue acknowledge that Jesus Christ is Lord, to the glory of God the Father. (Philippians 2:9-11)

Even though we're all accountable, God has never forced us to obey Him, He has given us free choice. Even when He brought the Israelites out of Egypt with His mighty hand and led them to Canaan, overthrowing their enemies and warning them not to follow any other gods, He still gave them a choice.

> Now fear the LORD and serve him with all faithfulness. Throw away the gods your ancestors worshipped beyond the Euphrates River and in Egypt, and serve the LORD. But if serving the

Mankind

> LORD seems undesirable to you, choose for yourselves this day whom you will serve, whether the gods your ancestors served beyond the Euphrates, or the gods of the Amorites, in whose land you are living. But as for me and my household, we will serve the LORD. (Joshua 24:14-15)

We either serve God or not.

It's not the desire of God anyone should perish.

> The Lord is not slow in keeping his promise, as some understand slowness.
>
> He is patient with you, not wanting anyone to perish, but everyone to come to repentance. (2 Peter 3:9)

As for the servants who do heed the call of the Holy Spirit, they are promised blessings beyond measure.

> I pray that out of his glorious riches he may strengthen you with power through his Spirit in your inner being, so that Christ may dwell in your hearts through faith.
>
> And I pray that you, being rooted and established in love, may have power, together with all the Lord's holy people, to grasp how wide and long and high and deep is the love of Christ, and to know this love that surpasses knowledge – that you may be filled to the measure of all the fullness of God.
>
> Now to him who is able to do immeasurably more than all we ask or imagine, according to his power that is at work within us. (Ephesians 3:16-20)

Mankind has been given the opportunity to respond to the message of the Holy Spirit and to go beyond the point of salvation from glory to glory.

> But we all, with open face beholding as in a glass the glory of the Lord, are changed into the same image from glory to glory, even as by the Spirit of the Lord. (2 Corinthians 3:18 KJV)

The servants within this parable represent all of mankind, because all of mankind will be accountable to God.

CHAPTER 5

The Works Required

The money given by the master was to enable his servants to carry out what he required. It was important the work the master required was carried out, and we see the dire consequences when it wasn't.

The work in the parable represents God's will for mankind. If man does not accomplish His will, nothing less than the wrath of God awaits them, followed by eternal damnation.

Accomplishing God's will within our lives becomes very important and the Bible makes this fact very clear.

What is the will of God?

Jesus makes clear the fundamental requirements of His Father's will.

> For I have come down from heaven not to do my will but to do the will of him who sent me. And this is the will of him who sent me, that I shall lose none of all those he has given me, but raise them up at the last day.
>
> For my Father's will is that everyone who looks to the Son and believes in him shall have eternal life, and I will raise them up at the last day. (John 6:38-40)

The fundamental requirement of God's will is to believe and accept Jesus Christ as Lord of our lives. Which means we're turning from our life independent of God, to becoming dependent on Christ.

More than salvation is required of Christians. We start to see the difference between the two faithful servants who were given two and five talents. In the parable in Luke 19:11-26, the two faithful servants accomplished different results, one five minas and the other ten minas.

For Christians, this (usually overlooked) factor becomes very important. The Bible continually addresses this predicament throughout its pages from Genesis through to Revelation. The Bible is written to encourage servants to become the receivers of five talents and producers of ten minas.

What is there beyond salvation?

I will quote some of the many Scriptures pointing us toward the servants who will achieve the most. And you will start to understand why this parable is important. It demonstrates the desire Christ has for His believers.

> Jesus replied, 'Anyone who loves me will obey my teaching. My Father will love them, and we will come to them and make our home with them.' (John 14:23)

> He said to them all: 'Whoever wants to be my disciple must deny themselves and take up their cross daily and follow me. For whoever wants to save their life will lose it, but whoever loses their life for me will save it.' (Luke 9:23-24)

> As for everyone who comes to me and hears my words and puts them into practice, I will show you what they are like. They are like a man building a house, who dug down deep and laid the foundation on rock.

When a flood came, the torrent struck the house but could not shake it, because it was well built. (Luke 6:47-48)

For we're God's handiwork, created in Christ Jesus to do good works, which God prepared in advance for us to do. (Ephesians 2:10)

Do not conform to the pattern of this world, but be transformed by the renewing of your mind. You will be able to test and approve what God's will is – his good, pleasing and perfect will. (Romans 12:2)

Lord, who may dwell in your sacred tent? Who may live on your holy mountain? The one whose walk is blameless, who does what is righteous, who speaks the truth from their heart, whose tongue utters no slander, who does no wrong to a neighbour, and casts no slur on others; who despises a vile person but honours those who fear the LORD; who keeps an oath even when it hurts, and does not change their mind; who lends money to the poor without interest, who does not accept a bribe against the innocent. Whoever does these things will never be shaken. (Psalm 15)

These are a tiny portion of the scriptures encouraging us to be Five Talent Servants.

CHAPTER 6

The Significance of the Talents and Minas

If the Holy Spirit represents the talents and minas, we can have a better appreciation of why this becomes very significant. When the talents and the minas are distributed, both masters require results.

Even when the money isn't put into use, they expected the servant to at least put it into the bank to receive interest. Why is this important? Why is it relevant to us?

When the Holy Spirit moves throughout mankind, good fruit is expected to be produced.

> Anyone who speaks a word against the Son of Man will be forgiven, but anyone who speaks against the Holy Spirit will not be forgiven, either in this age or in the age to come.
> Make a tree good and its fruit will be good, or make a tree bad and its fruit will be bad, for a tree is recognised by its fruit.
> (Matthew 12:32)

Here we see, if we do not heed the Holy Spirit, or speak against the Holy Spirit, no good fruit can be produced with disastrous consequences.

The axe is already at the root of the trees, and every tree that does not produce good fruit will be cut down and thrown into the fire. (Matthew 3:10)

The Holy Spirit is given so we may produce good fruit.

> By their fruit you will recognise them. Do people pick grapes from thorn bushes, or figs from thistles?
>
> Likewise, every good tree bears good fruit, but a bad tree bears bad fruit. A good tree cannot bear bad fruit, and a bad tree cannot bear good fruit.
>
> Every tree that does not bear good fruit is cut down and thrown into the fire. Thus, by their fruit you will recognise them. (Matthew 3:16-20)

The good fruit is the will of God. Not only is there a basic requirement (Ephesians 1:13[1]), but there is spiritual growth and maturity beyond salvation.

We can see three different levels within these two parables.

In both parables concerning the Talents and the Minas, there is a difference between each of the three levels. To make this clearer, we need to see why the three different results play a vital role in understanding what these parables are pointing us toward.

Within the parable of the talents, the distribution is different, five, two and one. Within the parable of the minas, the distribution is equal but the results are different, tenfold, fivefold and none.

Was the initial distribution equal? The answer is yes. You may argue, 'but the distribution of the Talents was not equal.'

This is where the consistency of God's Word becomes important.

---

1 'And you also were included in Christ when you heard the message of truth, the gospel of your salvation. When you believed, you were marked in him with a seal, the promised Holy Spirit.'

If you come across a Scripture that doesn't make sense, always understand, the Bible will never contradict its fundamental doctrine, it's always consistent.

The one talent and the ten minas represent God's Spirit giving mankind the ability to know Him.

The opportunity for mankind to come into the kingdom of God, is available to all.

> But very truly I tell you, it is for your good that I am going away. Unless I go away, the Advocate (Holy Spirit) will not come to you; but if I go, I will send him to you.
>
> When he comes, he will prove the world to be in the wrong about sin and righteousness and judgment: about sin, because people do not believe in me; about righteousness, because I am going to the Father, where you can see me no longer, and about judgement, because the prince of this world stands condemned. (John 16:7-11)

The Holy Spirit has come to reveal our sins are forgiven through Jesus Christ, and God has accepted His Son's full payment for the sins of the world by the cross setting us free through His righteousness, because He is seated at the right hand of His Father.

Through Christ, our condemnation is removed, giving us the ability to resist the devil.

It's the desire of God all should come into His kingdom.

> The Lord is not slow in keeping his promise, as some understand slowness. Instead he is patient with you, not wanting anyone to perish, but everyone to come to repentance. (2 Peter 3:9)

This has always been the desire of God.

> For since the creation of the world God's invisible qualities – his eternal power and divine nature – have been clearly seen, being understood from what has been made, so people are without excuse. (Romans 1:20)

There will always be debates and arguments about the gospel not reaching everyone, but the Bible makes it very clear, no one will have an excuse when they stand before Him. The one talent or the ten minas represent the Spirit going throughout the world, giving man the opportunity to respond to His calling.

This still doesn't answer the giving of the talents unequally. The parable in Luke 19:11-13 gives them equality, but the parable in Matthew 25:14-15 does not. To clarify this, we need to look carefully at the wording.

> And unto one he gave five talents, to another two, and to another one, to every man according to his several abilities, and straight away took his journey. (Matthew 25:15 KJV)

This is easy to sort out because the master already knew where each of his servants were at. Two of his servants had already proven to be obedient to what he required.

We come to the Two Talent Servant. This is an important factor within this parable and the reason I wrote this book.

The Two Talent Servant and the servant who produced five minas represent the majority of Christians in this world. Both are commended by their master and are rewarded for their faithful obedience. Yet both never get more fruit (Matthew 25:28-29, Luke 19:24-26).

The Two Talent Servant does make a gain on what he is given. What makes the Two Talent Servant different from the Five Talent Servant?

The Significance of the Talents and Minas

What is the fundamental requirement of Christianity? As we have seen, God requires good fruit. What is the basic requirement of God?

> For God so loved the world He gave His one and only Son, that whoever believes in Him shall not perish but have eternal life.
> For God did not send his Son into the world to condemn the world, but to save the world through Him. Whoever believes in Him is not condemned, but whoever does not believe stands condemned already because they have not believed in the name of God's one and only Son. (John 3:16-18)

This is the basic requirement of God for all who hear His words. The Two Talent Servant and the servant who produced five minas represent all who have believed, repented and accepted Jesus Christ as Lord.

They have become faithful servants, but in both parables, their fruit isn't added to.

Through this parable, God highlighted this particular servant.

In 1997 I had already been a Christian for nine years, but I knew in my heart, I wasn't where God wanted me. My heart wasn't fully surrendered to Him. I knew I belonged to God through Christ, but I was living a mediocre Christian life.

I was dissatisfied in my heart where I was with the Lord and was not including Christ in all areas of my life.

At this time the Holy Spirit told me to 'press in' with a full surrendering of my heart. Even though my destiny was heavenly, God didn't want me to stay in the state I was in.

He wanted me to experience His fullness which brings a solid foundation withstanding the storms of this world.

It wasn't long after this the parable of the talents became one of those passages of Scripture I couldn't gloss over. I knew in my spirit the Lord was wanting to highlight some truths within that were not easily seen.

It was the Two Talent Servant who was highlighted. I became aware I was the Two Talent Servant and God wanted me to move beyond this realm and into the realm of the Five Talent Servant.

The Two Talent Servant represents all born-again Christians who are still compromising with the world and sin, who are making excuses for the shortcomings, who do not quite fully trust God. They are resigned to this being as good as it's going to get, they doubt whether they can go beyond where they find themselves. They remain stuck in this realm.

But those who are dissatisfied with this and believe God can move them forward, move into the Five Talent Servant realm.

This brings us to the Five Talent Servant. This is the realm the Bible shines its light on. Scripture speaks directly to five talent servants and five talent servants operate in it.

This is where the Holy Spirit desires to lead all of God's servants, but it comes at a cost and we can slip in and out of this realm.

Once you view Scripture through these eyes, you come to realise the Word of God gives us the ability to live in and experience all the Bible boldly has for us.

Chapter 7

The Hard Task Master

> He who had received the one talent came and said, Lord, I knew thee that thou art an hard man, reaping where thou hast not sown, and gathering where thou hast not strawed. (Matthew 25:24 KJV)

> I was afraid of you, because you are a hard man. You take out what you did not put in and reap what you did not sow. (Luke 19:21)

These particular verses put us in a peculiar theological conundrum. They are suggesting the servants, in their own efforts, have to break new ground the master hasn't broken and the master will get the profit.

The spiritual meaning suggests this: God requires us to break new ground He hasn't broken and He will get the benefit.

Here's the conundrum. The Bible makes it absolutely clear, mankind can never gain God's favour by his own efforts.

> For it is by grace you have been saved, through faith – this is not from yourselves, it is the gift of God – not by works, so none can boast. For we're God's handiwork, created in Christ Jesus

to do good works, which God prepared in advance for us to do. (Ephesians 2:8)

The Bible says our salvation is through Jesus and the good works we accomplish are through Jesus, leaving us with nothing to boast about. Every good thing we accomplish in God, is through God and not ourselves.

How can these parables suggest we're breaking ground God hasn't broken?

Is the Bible contradicting itself?

No.

The servants were given talents and minas, therefore the Holy Spirit is still involved and the Spirit gives us the ability to break new ground. But we must be clear the new ground broken is required from us and neither God or the Son or the Holy Spirit can do it for us.

There is a statement Jesus makes bringing a solution to this problem and proving the harmony of Scripture.

> He said to them all: 'Whoever wants to be my disciple must deny themselves and take up their cross daily and follow me.
> 'For whoever wants to save their life will lose it, but whoever loses their life for me will save it.' (Luke 9:23-24)

First, we're to repent and surrender to the Lordship of Christ, and as children of God, we're to surrender to the Lordship of Christ.

To follow Christ is voluntary, and God will never force Himself or His ways upon us. Choice is what God has left to us. But to choose Christ involves a cost to our flesh.

This is the new ground God hasn't broken that must be broken. The choice belongs to us. We must make the decision whether we die to ourselves and let Christ reign, or not.

Not only must the decision be made at the point of salvation, but it must be continually made throughout our Christian lives.

On our own, we don't have the ability to choose.

> As it is written: 'There is no one righteous, not even one; there is no one who understands; there is no one who seeks God. All have turned away, they have together become worthless; there is no one who does good, not even one.' (Romans 3:10-13)

The Holy Spirit is involved to take away the deception so we can make the vital choice. It's still entirely our choice.

The breaking of new ground is the dying to self so Christ may reign there in our stead. Whenever we die to self, this is the breaking of new ground God hasn't broken and it needs to be broken.

This is the dilemma mankind has vehemently fought against since the fall of man. To give up our rights to be lord of our own lives and hand it over to the Lord Jesus Christ is too costly for many.

Most of mankind choose to bury this truth and reject God.

An excellent illustration of this is found in the parable of the sower and the seed found in Matthew 13:3-8, 18-23, Mark 4:3-8, 14-20, Luke 8:5-8, 11-15. In this parable, we see seed falling on different types of land, on the hard path, on rocky places, among thorns and on good soil.

The land represents our hearts or more succinctly, it represents how willing we're to die to self. This parable makes it clear a totally surrendered heart is the only soil able to produce abundantly.

The dying of self is the one thing God has left up to us. He will reveal the truth to us through the Holy Spirit, but it's still up to us whether we're prepared to break the ground for the glory of God and not ourselves.

We have seen what is represented in these parables, let's look at who these three servants represent.

PART 2
The One Talent Servant

Chapter 8

Introducing the One Talent Servant

The sad reality about this life is sin exists, and worse, people choose to stay under its grip. Sin is the reason we're separated from God. And if we're separated from God, we can't follow the will of God.

One Talent Servants do not represent the least in the kingdom of God. No, they represent all those who are not part of God's kingdom, because they have failed to do what was required.

God doesn't remain silent or hidden. Through many different ways, He makes Himself known and all are without excuse. Romans 1:20 'For since the creation of the world God's invisible qualities – his eternal power and divine nature – have been clearly seen, being understood from what has been made, so people are without excuse.'

God sent His Son so all who believe in Him will not perish, but all those who reject this, will be condemned.

> For God so loved the world, He gave his only begotten Son, that whosoever believeth in him should not perish, but have everlasting life.
>
> For God sent not his Son into the world to condemn the world; but that the world through him might be saved. He that believeth on him is not condemned: but he that believeth not is condemned already, because he hath not believed in the name of the only begotten Son of God. (John 3:16-18 KJV)

First we see God has made Himself known through creation itself, man has had no excuse for not knowing Him. The reason they didn't is because they suppressed the truth.

> For although they knew God, they neither glorified him as God nor gave thanks to him, but their thinking became futile and their foolish hearts were darkened. (Romans 1:21)

He sent His Son to put an end to sin for those who believe in Him, they are given the right to become children of God. All those who reject this, reject it because they prefer the darkness outside God, rather than the light Christ brings.

> This is the verdict: Light has come into the world, but people loved darkness instead of light because their deeds were evil. Everyone who does evil hates the light, and will not come into the light for fear their deeds will be exposed. (John 3:19-20)

Here we see God isn't inactive but the opposite. It's not because mankind didn't know God, it's because mankind didn't want to know God.

When Jesus came into the world, He was the light and shone upon the darkness. Many rejected Him, not because they didn't know who He was, but because they preferred their own darkness to His light.

Jesus is the true Light, but many reject this Light because it exposes their wicked ways and amplifies their depravity compared to His brilliant Light.

These are the ones who refuse to do what God requires of them, they are the One Talent Servants and there are many reasons, but we will look at only a few to make this clear.

CHAPTER 9

Refusing to Submit

In both parables, the servant who buries the money also complains about how the master is an unjust task master.

> ...he who had received the one talent came and said, Lord, I knew thee that thou art an hard man, reaping where thou hast not sown, and gathering where thou hast not strawed: And I was afraid, and went and hid thy talent in the earth: lo, there thou hast that is thine. (Matthew 25:24-25 KJV)

This is the same response of the servant in Luke 19:21.

What do these passages mean and what have they got to do with submission?

The reaction of these disobedient servants echoes throughout the Scriptures and is one of the biggest reasons the majority of mankind stay outside God's kingdom.

We need to remember, these disobedient men were first of all servants. Servants are accountable to their master. All of mankind is accountable to God.

The reason we're born is to come to know our Lord and Saviour. This has been God's will from the very beginning, but because of sin, a wall has come in between, seemingly impossible to breach.

This sin has made man fiercely independent from God and

unwilling to submit. Because of this fierce independence, mankind chooses to remain in the dark.

> In the beginning was the Word, and the Word was with God, and the Word was God. The same was in the beginning with God. All things were made by him; and without him was not anything made that was made. In him was life; and the life was the light of men. And the light shineth in darkness; and the darkness comprehended it not. That was the true Light, which lighteth every man that cometh into the world. He was in the world, and the world was made by him, and the world knew him not. (John 1:1-5, 9-10 KJV)

Jesus the Messiah came into the world, but because of people's darkened hearts, they chose to reject the true Light. They didn't recognise the Messiah because of the condition of their hearts.

> This is the verdict: Light has come into the world, but people loved darkness instead of light because their deeds were evil. Everyone who does evil hates the light, and will not come into the light for fear that their deeds will be exposed. (John 3:19-20)

Because of sin, mankind has become fiercely independent from God and has been deceived into the world of darkness. Jesus came so mankind could be saved from this darkness, but they didn't want to come out of the darkness and their sinful nature was not willing to let them.

This is where people cry out that God has made it unjust and is a hard task master. Jesus tackles this problem head-on in Luke 9:23-24,

> He said to them all: 'Whoever wants to be my disciple must

deny themselves and take up their cross daily and follow me. For whoever wants to save their life will lose it, but whoever loses their life for me will save it.'

God requires nothing less than full surrender of our lives and this is something we have to choose. It's only through the Holy Spirit we're brought to this place, but it's something God can't force us to do.

This is where freedom of choice determines our destiny.

It's not what we have accomplished by our own strength, or righteousness, but the power of God leading us to a cross-road in our lives giving us the opportunity to make a choice whether to surrender to the Lord Jesus Christ or not.

Surrendering to the Lord Jesus means breaking ground that has never been broken, and it has to be done by us. This ground is dying to our sinful independent lives.

This is something God requires all of mankind to make, unfortunately, most people are not willing to make the sacrifice. They make many excuses; they moan, they ignore, they spit back, they bury, they laugh, they joke, they scorn, they hate, they run from, they protest, they discourage others, they rebel.

They have no need of such sacrifice. They are fiercely independent, they love the darkness, they hate the Light, they don't want to die to self. This list could continue, emphasising the many examples of man's response to God's call.

After we have surrendered our lives to Christ Jesus, it's not us getting the glory, but God. We're to die to our lives so Christ may be glorified.

To a Christian, this makes sense because we know how God operates and the benefits we receive, but non-Christians find this too hard to fathom.

When the servant came back and said to his master, 'I knew that you are a hard man, harvesting where you have not sown and gathering where you have not scattered seed.' (Matthew 25:24)

This is the response mankind shows God concerning His will for them to surrender to Him through His Son. They are unwilling to pay such a costly sacrifice involving removing 'self' off the throne and allowing Christ to reign there and allow Christ to gain the glory, and not ourselves.

It's understandable why most of the world still lives in darkness.

CHAPTER 10

Burying the Truth

> 'And I was afraid, and went and hid thy talent in the earth: lo, there thou hast that is thine.' (Matthew 25:25 KJV)

The NIV says,

> So I was afraid and went out and hid your gold in the ground. See, here is what belongs to you.

A few questions need to be asked here, plus, what light does this shed on the condition of mankind?

- Why did fear motivate this?
- Why did he bury the money (talents)?
- Why did he keep it, and return it?
- What has all this got to do with fallen man?

The first question addresses fear. This isn't biblical fear where the Bible says in Psalms 111:10,

> The fear of the LORD is the beginning of wisdom…

No, this is the type of fear driving a person away from God, not toward Him.

Here we see the servant is afraid of what is required of him. The master wants the servant to break new ground and the harvest going to the master.

The master has already made it clear what was required of the servants due to the obedience of the other two. This servant who received the one talent, was not prepared to obey his master's instructions. This servant was not prepared to put in the work required because the benefit went to the master and not him.

He was afraid because he felt strongly what the master required of him was unjust and of no benefit to him. The sacrifice on his behalf was too great and he foresaw no immediate benefit for himself.

The servants could only reap the benefits when the master returned. This fear left him with the inability to do what was required.

This attitude is another reason most of the world is outside God's kingdom. God has made it clear what is required of mankind.

> The wrath of God is being revealed from heaven against all the godlessness and wickedness of people, who suppress the truth by their wickedness, since what may be known about God is plain to them, because God has made it plain to them. For since the creation of the world God's invisible qualities – his eternal power and divine nature – have been clearly seen, being understood from what has been made, so people are without excuse. (Romans 1:18-20)

God's desire is for all of mankind to come to know Him.

For God so loved the world He gave his one and only Son,

whoever believes in him shall not perish but have eternal life. (John 3:16)

And He desires none perish:

> The Lord is not slow in keeping his promise, as some understand slowness. He is patient with you, not wanting anyone to perish, but everyone to come to repentance. (2 Peter 3:9)

Here is the part making mankind afraid.

> He called the crowd to him along with his disciples and said: 'Whoever wants to be my disciple must deny themselves and take up their cross and follow me. For whoever wants to save their life will lose it, but whoever loses their life for me and for the gospel will save it.' (Mark 8:34-35)

This is the ground Christ requires us to break, we're to lay our lives down for the Lord Jesus. We're no longer in charge, He is. Not our will, but His will.

We have to trust Him when He leads us through triumphs and tribulations. The glory goes to Him and not us. It's nothing short of death to self so Christ Jesus may reign within our lives.

We become accountable to God.

Giving up this independence isn't something mankind is willing to do, and refuses to do. Even when the Holy Spirit is involved in this process.

This leads to the next question. Why did he bury the money (talent)? He buried the money because it belonged to the master and he knew he had to return it. He also buried it because he didn't want to be reminded of what was required.

When people reject the calling of God, it's not as if this leaves them alone from now on. No, this calling will cross their paths many times.

But because they embrace darkness rather than the light, this truth is buried or suppressed.

> The wrath of God is being revealed from heaven against all the godlessness and wickedness of people, who suppress the truth by their wickedness. (Romans 1:18)

People reject God because they are afraid of what is required – to become accountable to God Almighty through Jesus Christ. This rejection is wilful, and, in turn, suppresses the Truth.

Because most of mankind has rejected the Truth, they try and bury it. This Truth will never go away, but fallen man is always trying to suppress this truth. Individually and collectively, man would generally bury this truth rather than do what God requires.

This brings us to the question – why did he keep and return the money?

The talents or money given represents the Holy Spirit. This money could never be used for anything but the Master's requirements. The talent given made the servant accountable to the master.

God makes Himself known through the Holy Spirit, and the Spirit goes throughout the world revealing the truth to mankind.

> But very truly I tell you, it is for your good that I am going away.
> Unless I go away, the Advocate will not come to you; but if I go, I will send him to you. When he comes, he will prove the world to be in the wrong about sin and righteousness and judgement. (John 16:7-8)

Man will be held accountable for what has been given. Scripture tells us everyone will give an account before God.

It is written: 'As surely as I live,' says the Lord, 'every knee will bow before me; every tongue will acknowledge God.' (Romans 14:11-12)

Each of us will give an account of ourselves to God.

Mankind has been given the Truth and when we stand before God, we will have to give an account for the Truth.

The last question – what has all this got to do with fallen man? This has hopefully been made clear. This is the predicament of fallen man.

God has revealed Himself to all of mankind and has given us the ability to come to Him through His Son, the Lord Jesus Christ.

But mankind loved the darkness more, therefore rejected the Truth and accepted the lie. To live this lie, he has to bury the Truth.

When we meet our death, we will be accountable to our Creator and Master and be asked, what have we done with the Truth?

Where did we bury it?

Chapter 11

Bearing Fruit

Bearing fruit is important to God, so important we're warned if we bear no fruit we will be cast out.

There are many verses in the Bible saying this. If no fruit is being produced in our lives, the Bible makes it clear what happens.

This is John the Baptist rebuking the religious rulers of Israel:

> Produce fruit in keeping with repentance. The axe is already at the root of the trees, and every tree that does not produce good fruit will be cut down and thrown into the fire. (Matthew 3:10,12)

Jesus says the same thing:

> Every tree that bringeth not forth good fruit is hewn down, and cast into the fire. Wherefore by their fruits ye shall know them. (Matthew 7:19-20 KJV)

The next passage of Scripture is probably the best description of why bearing fruit is so important.

> I am the true vine, and my Father is the gardener. He cuts off every branch in me that bears no fruit, while every branch that does bear fruit he prunes so it will be even more fruitful.

> You are already clean because of the word I have spoken to you. Remain in me, as I also remain in you. No branch can bear fruit by itself, it must remain in the vine. Neither can you bear fruit unless you remain in me.
>
> I am the vine; you are the branches. If you remain in me and I in you, you will bear much fruit; apart from me you can do nothing. If you do not remain in me, you are like a branch that is thrown away and withers; such branches are picked up, thrown into the fire and burned. (John 15:1-5)

What has this got to do with the 'One Talent Servant'?

This is the reason the master threw him into the outer darkness. The master required results from what was given and expected nothing less. This was not unfair, because the servant was accountable to the master, plus he was shown what was required of him.

What has God required of us by what He has given?

The most basic requirement is justification by faith. This theme has run throughout the whole Bible. Faith is believing and obeying the instruction of the Holy Spirit.

People of faith believed God and this set them apart. This meant during Old Testament times, only a remnant of Israel belonged to God.

> It is not as though God's word had failed. For not all who are descended from Israel are Israel.
>
> Nor because they are his descendants are they all Abraham's children. On the contrary, 'It is through Isaac that your offspring will be reckoned.' (Romans 9:6-8)

In other words, it is not the children of physical descent who are God's children, but it is the children of the promise who are regarded as Abraham's offspring.

What was said to Abraham that was of great importance to God?

For what saith the scripture? Abraham believed God, and it was counted unto him for righteousness. (Romans 4:3 KJV)

Therefore, the promise comes by faith, so that it may be by grace and may be guaranteed to all Abraham's offspring – not only to those who are of the law but also to those who have the faith of Abraham. He is the father of us all. (Romans 4:16)

Here we see, faith in God is the key factor. All who believed and obeyed God were the True Israel. And this faith continues on through Jesus Christ, so both Jew and Gentile who believe and obey the Lord Jesus Christ become children of God.

God sent His Son so we might become His children because of what Jesus accomplished on the cross. The basic requirement is this:

For God so loved the world that he gave his one and only Son, that whoever believes in him shall not perish but have eternal life. (John 3:16 KJV)

The fruit required for us is represented by the 'Two Talent' and the 'Five Talent Servants', and this is to become children of God.

But as many as received him, to them gave the power to become the sons of God, even to them that believe on his name: who were born, not of blood, nor of the will of the flesh, nor of the will of man, but of God. (John 1:12-13 KJV)

'So in Christ Jesus you are all children of God through faith, for all of you who were baptised into Christ have clothed yourselves with Christ.' (Galatians 3:25-26)

To Be a Five Talent Servant

The One Talent Servant of Matthew 25:30[2] represents all who have not believed and obeyed what the Holy Spirit has instructed. And since the death and resurrection of Jesus Christ, the requirement of God is to believe and obey His Son, which has been rejected by all who are represented by the One Talent Servant.

The servants of Matthew and Luke who failed to produce anything for their masters were both punished severely. Mankind is accountable to our Creator and if we do not bear the fruit required, we will be severely punished.

---

2 'And cast ye the unprofitable servant into outer darkness: there shall be weeping and gnashing of teeth.'

PART 3

The Two Talent Servant

CHAPTER 12

Introducing the Two Talent Servant

It was understanding the Two Talent Servant which played a major part in this book being written.

This servant isn't noticed as much as the other two servants, yet this servant represents many Christians.

This servant is good and faithful and is commended by his master as such. He is given responsibility in his kingdom. But as we look closer, we see things making this servant different to the Five Talent Servant.

First, the Five Talent Servant is given more than what he already has by the master. The Bible says in Matthew 25:29 (KJV),

> For unto every one that hath shall be given, and he shall have abundance…

Again in Luke 19:26,

> He replied, 'I tell you that to everyone who has, more will be given…'

Ever noticed the Two Talent Servant and the servant who achieved a 50 percent profit isn't mentioned by the master as 'one who has'? This middle servant isn't given more.

These two servants within these parables are easily overlooked when the Lord was highlighting the parable of the talents many years ago.

It was the Two Talent Servant I felt in my heart the Lord was wanting me to understand.

The Two Talent Servant is safe within the kingdom of God, but it's not where God wants us to remain.

At the time the Holy Spirit was highlighting this particular parable in my life, a big change had happened spiritually. I became a Christian in 1988 and I had been walking with the Lord for nine years when a spiritual turning point happened in 1997.

During the years leading up to this time, I knew I was a child of our Heavenly Father through Christ. There was no desire within this period for me to go back to the world and place my trust there. I knew in my heart I loved the Lord and I really did want to please Him.

But there was a problem.

To get straight to the heart of it, I was not fully surrendered nor did I want to be. I had a mediocre relationship with the Lord. And because of this, there were many areas in my life the Holy Spirit wasn't able to bring victory or wisdom.

In the parable of Matthew 25, God was showing me I was that Two Talent Servant, but He didn't want me to remain there. Even though we will experience God's Presence in our lives, it never feels like the full potential due to the compromises in our lives.

There are many reasons we remain Two Talent Servants, and there is a common thread letting us know where we stand. That thread is a dissatisfaction in our hearts from where we're at with our relationship with our Lord and Saviour.

There is a desire to honour Him, but there is always something knocking it back. The desire is proof the Holy Spirit is active within, but the knock-backs are proof we continue to contend with and often fail against our fleshy nature, our spiritual enemies and the world and its pattern.

Chapter 13

Who are Two Talent Servants?

All Two Talent Servants have received Jesus Christ as their Lord and Saviour. They all have the Holy Spirit dwelling inside them. All Two Talent servants have a desire to please God.

They can be found among new believers, right through to the veterans of the faith.

Because they have accepted Jesus Christ as Saviour, they have fulfilled the basic requirements of Almighty God. Their names have been written in the Lamb's Book of Life. The indwelling Holy Spirit makes their salvation secure.

There is a thread running through all Two Talent Servants separating them from Five Talent Servants.

> He said to them all: 'Whoever wants to be my disciple must deny themselves and take up their cross daily and follow me. For whoever wants to save their life will lose it, but whoever loses their life for me will save it.' (Luke 9:23-24)

The common thread among Two Talent Servants is these verses are not being fulfilled in some areas of their lives. There is a dissatisfaction in their hearts because they seem to continually fall short or get taken away from Christ's path. Or are plagued by a particular sin.

All Two Talent Servants know in their hearts they are falling short of where they should be. For some reason there is an area in their lives they can't completely die to and trust God with. Whether it's an ingrained sin or a temptation that doesn't want to be let go. Or the busyness of life crowds out our time with Christ.

There are many factors causing us to be Two Talent Servants. We can make excuses or we can accept this is the way it's going to remain. But a knowing in our hearts leaves us dissatisfied with where we are spiritually. That's a good thing, because it's the Holy Spirit being active in our lives.

This relationship with Christ is an Outer Courts relationship, but the Holy Spirit wants us to go into the Holy Place and further into the Most Holy Place on a regular basis.

Two Talent Servants may experience the Inner Courts, but it's usually a fleeting experience and not consistent.

Two Talent Servants will enter heaven, but there will be areas that will be burnt up before God.

> For no one can lay any foundation other than the one already laid, which is Jesus Christ. If anyone builds on this foundation using gold, silver, costly stones, wood, hay or straw, their work will be shown for what it is, because the Day will bring it to light. It will be revealed with fire, and the fire will test the quality of each person's work. If what has been built survives, the builder will receive a reward. If it is burned up, the builder will suffer loss but will be saved – even though only as one escaping through the flames. (1 Corinthians 3:11-15)

The following chapters are some of the reasons we remain Two Talent Servants.

Chapter 14

Our Gracious God

Before any subject is discussed concerning the faults of a Two Talent Servant, we need to understand God will continue to pour His love and acceptance upon us regardless of where we're spiritually.

As long as there is desire within, a heart wanting to do what's right and a longing for a deeper spiritual walk, God will meet us. In fact, God will pour into our lives far more abundantly than we deserve.

The Lord Jesus Christ understands the frailty of man and will strive with us, because we're connected to Him through the Holy Spirit. Even though His desire is for us to become completely free, throwing off the shackles holding us back, our Lord works with what He has. And He can work powerfully through our distorted lives.

Look closely at the people He used. Everyone who served Him was dysfunctional in some measure. They were people, like you and me.

We have a merciful God, and even though we know we let Him down on a regular basis, we never sense He has abandoned us. This is absolutely true, the Holy Spirit within will always encourage us to get back up, Christ will clean us up and we continue on.

If we could look back on our Christian walk and see all the times we failed to be obedient, we would be absolutely horrified.

But the Holy Spirit has continued to pour God's favour on our lives, Christ chooses to show up despite our failings. We experience the security of knowing we belong to God's family.

In short, God is more than willing to reveal Himself in us and through us far more than we deserve. This is what is so amazing. When we're not always faithful, God remains faithful to us.

> If we're faithless, he remains faithful, for he cannot disown himself. (2 Timothy 2:13)

If the Holy Spirit remains in us, we belong to God, and God can't disown Himself. Therefore, God will always remain active in us.

I write this chapter not to make us comfortable in our shortcomings, nor to feel ok about giving into sin. It's to remind us we really do serve a merciful and gracious God who will work with what He has and still do for us far greater than our true state deserves.

Since we have such a merciful and gracious God, let us throw off all that hinders us and run the race with freedom, unshackled.

The next chapters will deal with some of these shackles.

Chapter 15

Self-Righteousness Versus God's Righteousness

> What does Scripture say? 'Abraham believed God, and it was credited to him as righteousness.' Now to the one who works, wages are not credited as a gift but as an obligation. However, to the one who does not work but trusts God who justifies the ungodly, their faith is credited as righteousness. (Romans 4:3-5)

What kind of righteousness are we to live under? There are two kinds of righteousness in this world, self-righteousness and the Righteousness coming from God. This was a difficult deception God had to break in my life.

It's amazing what we're willing to believe and how we convince ourselves we're on the right track, even when we know something isn't working. God had to show me the difference between self-righteousness and His Righteousness.

To understand why self-righteousness is so dangerous and why we need to recognise it in our lives, we will look at three results of this sin. Self-righteousness will lead us on the path of pride, deception and blindness. We will see the extreme results of this, but it's only to make us aware how dangerous this path is, and we may not even realise we're on it.

First, we will look at self-righteousness feeding our pride.

To some who were confident of their own righteousness and looked down on everyone else, Jesus told this parable: 'Two men went up to the temple to pray, one a Pharisee and the other a tax collector. The Pharisee stood by himself and prayed. "God, I thank you that I am not like other people – robbers, evildoers, adulterers – or even like this tax collector. I fast twice a week and give a tenth of all I get."' (Luke 18:9-12)

When he noticed how the guests picked the places of honour at the table, he told them this parable: 'When someone invites you to a wedding feast, do not take the place of honour, for a person more distinguished than you may have been invited. If so, the host who invited both of you will come and say to you, "Give this person your seat."

'Humiliated, you will have to take the least important place. But when you are invited, take the lowest place, so that when your host comes, he will say to you, "Friend, move up to a better place."

'You will be honoured in the presence of all the other guests. For all those who exalt themselves will be humbled, and those who humble themselves will be exalted.' (Luke 14:7-11)

There are two areas of pride addressed here caused by self-righteousness. These are extreme cases of the righteousness of man. And often we humble Christians say to ourselves, 'I'm glad I'm not like the Pharisee announcing how righteous he is in public and glad I don't assume I deserve the place of honour all the time.'

Here is the scary fact: self-righteousness leads to that and often we become blind to the fact we're on that path. Whether we're at the beginning of the path, or whether we're on it without realising.

Pride will subtly convince us we're the one who has accomplished the good achieved in our lives. Pride doesn't even mind when we believe we're in partnership with Jesus Christ in achieving the good.

Pride is allowed to live when we allow credit to come back to ourselves. When we believe our righteousness makes us good. When we pat ourselves on the back for the good accomplished, this allows pride to bring recognition to ourselves.

Our righteousness is coming from ourselves. Usually this is never an over-the-top, full-blown Pharisaic pride, but believing pleasing God can come from our good, is on exactly the same path as the proud Pharisee.

One of the signs we can test ourselves, whether we rely on our righteousness or Christ's righteousness, is the failure or success of other brethren. When a brother or sister in the Lord falls, how does that make us feel? Does it make us feel good because it paints a better picture for ourselves? Or does it stir an understanding that only Christ's righteousness gives us the ability to stand, without which we're vulnerable?

When we see others being successful in the things of God, does it depress us because we're not so successful? Or are we happy because it's the Will of God at work?

Self-righteousness compares ourselves to others, God's Righteousness lets us see things through His eyes.

Every good we do and accomplish must glorify Jesus Christ and we must realise it's only because of Him we're able to do what is required. It's the righteousness of Christ giving us the ability to be righteous before God.

Understanding we're only righteous because of Christ's Holiness and not ours keeps us safe.

Another area of pride is believing we're someone special. This is a hard one to counter because the world celebrates this, and our society loves to recognise men and women of accomplishment.

When we credit our righteousness to ourselves, pride will make us feel important, it will tell us the accomplishment is our hard work and we deserve to be recognised.

The parable in Luke 14:7-11 has an important key to how we're to conduct ourselves everywhere we go.

> For all those who exalt themselves will be humbled, and those who humble themselves will be exalted. (Luke 14:11)

When Jesus washed the feet of His disciples (John 13:3-17), He was setting a standard for all Christians. We're called to walk in humility and not pride. This doesn't mean only operating at the lowest positions, it means we're to operate in a state of humility no matter what position we're in.

When we realise it's only through Jesus Christ, we're able to accomplish God's will, and we're able to hand the glory to Him. Everywhere we go, it's Christ who is the guest of honour, and we're to give Jesus the place of honour wherever we go and whatever we do.

Self-righteousness leads us to deception.

> Woe to you, teachers of the law and Pharisees, you hypocrites! You clean the outside of the cup and dish, but inside they are full of greed and self-indulgence. Blind Pharisee! First clean the inside of the cup and dish, and the outside also will be clean.
>
> Woe to you, teachers of the law and Pharisees, you hypocrites! You are like whitewashed tombs, beautiful on the outside but on the inside full of the bones of the dead and everything unclean. In the same way, on the outside you appear to people as righteous but on the inside you are full of hypocrisy and wickedness. (Matthew 23:25-28)

God's wrath is never more clearly demonstrated than here,

exposing the hypocrisy being covered up by self-righteousness. This deception is at its finest, giving the appearance of holiness, but within, unclean and unholy.

One of the most puzzling realities about Christians is we can hide sin and still appear righteous. From new-born Christians to seasoned believers, including leaders.

We're all vulnerable to this deception. If we allow this kind of self-righteousness to take full effect, we will end up like the Pharisees.

To counter deception, we need to walk in the light and not darkness.

> In him was life, and that life was the light of all mankind. The light shines in the darkness, and the darkness has not overcome it. (John 1:4-5)

Deception can only flourish when it remains hidden – only when it's brought into the light under the wise guidance of the Holy Spirit, can deception be truly dealt with.

Self-righteousness deceives in many ways, and one affecting me was a subtle form which deceives without us even realising.

One of the curses mankind is plagued with since the Fall is righteousness through merit. This kind of righteousness gives credit to ourselves and not God. All religions outside Christianity rely on this system.

It's when our life is put on a balance scale that the good and bad is measured, determining which will tip the scale. It's so prevalent, Christians are not immune to it. The Apostle Paul rebuked the Corinthian church for falling into this trap.

Our carnal fleshy nature defaults back to this if we're not careful.

The subtlety of this deception is powerful, it will lead us toward blatant sin and justify the sin. Merit-based righteousness either allows or compensates.

To allow is this, when we have been good for a while or done good deeds, temptations will whisper it's a reward. Or, it minimises the act of sin and reminds us we're good and this isn't going to affect us.

You still have to choose to step over the line. This is when self-righteousness becomes powerful and the Righteousness of Christ is ignored.

When we allow this, it puts us in the driving seat. There is a reason Jesus said, 'Take up your cross daily.' It's so we could lay down our self-righteousness and allow His power to take over.

It's only His Righteousness making us good. It's only His wisdom countering our deceptive way of thinking.

To compensate, we try to balance out the wrong with the good. When we do wrong, our guilt drives us to try and be better. Or we keep our outward appearance righteous, but are failing inwardly.

Either way, the reason we fail is because we're trying to be good in our own strength.

The only way to counter this is to cling on to Christ.

> Remain in me, as I also remain in you. No branch can bear fruit by itself; it must remain in the vine. Neither can you bear fruit unless you remain in me.
>
> I am the vine; you are the branches. It you remain in me and I in you, you will bear much fruit; apart from me you can do nothing. If you do not remain in me, you are like a branch that is thrown away and withers; such branches are picked up, thrown into the fire and burned.
>
> If you remain in me and my words remain in you, ask whatever you wish, and it will be done for you. (John 15:4-7)

This Scripture is telling us we need to actively surrender ourselves continually to the Lord Jesus Christ, so His strength accomplishes

His will. This is the only way we can counter the deception of self-righteousness. It also warns us about the dangers of trying to operate in our own strength.

Third, self-righteousness blinds us to the truth of Christ. Saul of Tarsus is a good example of what the righteousness of man accomplishes.

> ...though I myself have reasons for such confidence. If someone else thinks they have reasons to put confidence in the flesh, I have more: circumcised on the eighth day, of the people of Israel, of the tribe of Benjamin, a Hebrew of Hebrews; in regard to the law, a Pharisee; as for zeal, persecuting the church; as for righteousness based on the law, faultless. (Philippians 3:4-6)

This testimony alone should jolt us into the startling reality of mankind's inability to be righteous before God in their own strength. Here we have a zealous Israelite who is a successful active member of the Pharisees (who are extreme law-abiding Israelites who whole-heartily believe they are the true followers of the Holy Scriptures).

What is so startling about this testimony concerning Saul of Tarsus, is he was at the pinnacle of man's righteousness. He was the tip of the spear, leading the charge to defend the truth of God. In his zealousness to protect the truth, he persecuted what he thought was an anti-biblical cult who were known as 'The Way', or better known as 'Christians'.

There was no doubt about his sincerity. He believed 100 percent what he was doing was for God. Yet he was persecuting 'The Truth', Jesus Christ the true Messiah.

How could a man considered by his fellow Jewish compatriots to be an outstanding God-fearing righteous man get it so wrong?

Self-righteousness.

Whenever the Apostle Paul speaks of his past as Saul of Tarsus, he always notes his accomplishments came through his own efforts. He tried to follow and obey God in his own strength. He was trying to accomplish God's favour through his own abilities and efforts.

Unfortunately, this isn't an isolated case. We have a tendency to fall into this trap, even after we become Christians. Trying to please God in our own strength is part of the sin package passed down to us.

To earn God's favour is what our carnal fleshy nature desires, but it's devoid of God's Presence. This is why this particular sin blinds us to the truth.

When we're trying to be righteous before God in our own strength, the wisdom is imparted to us comes from ourselves or other sources, not directly from God.

If our truth isn't coming directly from the Holy Spirit, deception has room to manoeuvre. When deception takes its course, your truth becomes blind to 'The Truth'.

Saul of Tarsus knew Scripture better than most of his fellow Jews. When it came to obeying the Law (according to their standards), he was faultless. Even his genetic heritage was impressive, making him a Hebrew of Hebrews.

With all these facts seemingly in his favour, he completely missed the one truth the Old Testament continually underlined; The Lord Jesus Christ, the Messiah.

The Apostle Paul knew first-hand how dangerous this deception is, and it's in his Epistles we're told how to counter it.

> For it is written: 'I will destroy the wisdom of the wise; the intelligence of the intelligent I will frustrate.'
> Where is the wise person? Has not God made foolish the wisdom of the world? For since in the wisdom of God the world through its wisdom did not know him, God was pleased

through the foolishness of what was preached to save those who believe.

Jews demand signs and Greeks look for wisdom, but we preach Christ was crucified: a stumbling block to Jews and foolishness to Gentiles, but to those whom God has called, both Jews and Greeks, Christ the power of God and the wisdom of God.

For the foolishness of God is wiser than human wisdom, and the weakness of God is stronger than human strength. (1 Corinthians 1:19-25)

...know that a person is not justified by the works of the law, but by faith in Jesus Christ. So we, too, have put our faith in Christ Jesus that we may be justified by faith in Christ and not by the works of the law, because by the works of the law no one will be justified.

I have been crucified with Christ and I no longer live, but Christ lives in me. The life I now live in the body, I live by faith in the Son of God, who loved me and gave himself for me.

I do not set aside the grace of God, for if righteousness could be gained through the law, Christ died for nothing. (Galatians 2:16, 20-21)

...for it is God who works in you to will and to act in order to fulfil his good purpose. (Philippians 2:13)

We're to be covered by the Righteousness of Christ Jesus and not by our own righteousness.

Chapter 16

A Duel/Dual to the Death

The book of Romans is an excellent microcosm of the whole of the gospel, from the hopelessness of mankind to the successful and victorious life in Christ Jesus. It makes clear the position of mankind compared to the position of the Holy Almighty God. It tells us how this impossible gap is bridged and how to maintain a successful life through obedience to the Father, Son and the Holy Spirit.[3]

Chapter 7 of Romans is a pivotal chapter because it explains why we have this continual battle with sin even though we're new creations under the Lordship of Christ, with the indwelling of the Holy Spirit.

But before we look at chapter seven more closely, we need to establish how God brings mankind to Himself against impossible odds. And how He equips us to be victorious against impossible odds.

The first three chapters of Romans says emphatically how mankind both Jew and Gentile have all sinned and fallen short of the glory of God.

In chapter 1, Romans first addresses the condition of all mankind.

---

[3] This chapter is so important, a version of it is also included in my book, *God's Way to Success*. I am also writing a book on this subject.

> For since the creation of the world God's invisible qualities – his eternal power and divine nature – have been clearly seen, being understood from what has been made, so that people are without excuse. For although they knew God, they neither glorified him as God nor gave thanks to him, but their thinking became futile and their foolish hearts were darkened. (Romans 1:20-21)

Because mankind deliberately rejects God, He gives them over to deception which blinds them.

The Jews considered themselves separate from this debauchery and safe because they were descendants of Abraham and had the Law of Moses. They didn't bow down to detestable idols like the pagan Gentiles. But Paul makes it clear, they are in the same predicament as the Gentiles.

Romans says the Jews were unable to obey the righteous requirements of the Law in their own strength.

> You who boast in the law, do you dishonour God by breaking the law? As it is written: 'God's name is blasphemed among the Gentiles because of you.' (Romans 2:23-24)

The Jews tried to obey God in their own strength, disconnecting them from God. The Jews had rejected God.

The Bible says both Jew and Gentile operating in their own strength can't obey God.

> What shall we conclude? Do we have any advantage? Not at all! For we have already made the charge that Jews and Gentiles alike are all under the power of sin.
>
>   As it is written: 'There is no one righteous, not even one; there is no one who understands; there is no one who seeks God. All

have turned away, they have together become worthless; there is no one who does good, not even one.' (Romans 3:9-12)

Romans chapters 4 and 5, brings the answer to this dire situation for mankind.

It's through faith, righteousness is imparted to us. Romans chapter 4 clearly shows it has always been faith that pleases God.

We need to understand clearly what Biblical faith is. Faith must include both God and man. Faith is believing and obeying the instruction of the Holy Spirit.

> And without faith it is impossible to please God, because anyone who comes to him must believe that he exists and that he rewards those who earnestly seek him. (Hebrews 11:6)

Faith is the Holy Spirit at work giving us the ability to believe and obey. To believe wholeheartedly and to obey unreservedly.

It's by faith and not our works, which God requires.

> If, in fact, Abraham was justified by works, he had something to boast about – but not before God. What does Scripture say? 'Abraham believed God, and it was credited to him as righteousness.' (Romans 4:2-3)

> Therefore, the promise comes by faith, so that it may be by grace and may be guaranteed to all Abraham's offspring – not only to those who are of the law but also to those who have the faith of Abraham. He is the father of us all. (Romans 4:16)

Romans chapter 5 says it's faith in Jesus Christ imparting God's righteousness.

> Therefore, since we have been justified through faith, we have peace with God through our Lord Jesus Christ, through whom we have gained access by faith into this grace in which we now stand. And we boast in the hope of the glory of God. (Romans 5:1-2)

We're put right before God through Jesus Christ.

> But God demonstrates his own love for us in this: While we were still sinners, Christ died for us. Since we have been justified by his blood, how much more shall we be saved from God's wrath through him! (Romans 5:8-9)

It's through faith alone we're justified before God and are welcomed into His family.

Now we're accepted, the Bible shows a radical new reality for us we may find hard to believe. Romans chapter 6 clearly tells us the results of our faith in Christ. If we truly believe Scripture this chapter, and many others throughout the Bible make some startling statements.

It says as born again, new creations, we're no longer subject to sin.

> …We're those who have died to sin; how can we live in it any longer? (Romans 6:2)

When Jesus died on the cross, He conquered sin once and for all. When we're born again, we experience the same.

> Or don't you know all of us who were baptised into Christ Jesus were baptised into his death? We were therefore buried with him through baptism into death in order that, as Christ was

raised from the dead through the glory of the Father, we too may live a new life.

For if we have been united with him in a death like his, we will certainly also be united with him in a resurrection like his. For we know that our old self was crucified with him so that the body ruled by sin might be done away with, that we should no longer be slaves to sin – because anyone who has died has been set free from sin. (Romans 6:3-7)

The Bible says we no longer sin because we're in Christ Jesus who has conquered sin and does not submit to it.
Do we believe this?
This point is made clear again in Romans 6:10-11,

The death he died, he died to sin once for all; but the life he lives, he lives to God. In the same way, count yourselves dead to sin but alive to God in Christ Jesus.

Do we really understand what the Bible is declaring here? We no longer have to submit to sin because we're already victorious in Christ.
The Bible emphasises this point.

But thanks be to God, though you used to be slaves to sin, you have come to obey from your heart the pattern of teaching that has now claimed your allegiance. You have been set free from sin and have become slaves to righteousness. (Romans 6:17-18)

Are we slaves to righteousness? Probably, no? So, who is wrong here, the Bible or us? Is the Bible wrong or is our understanding of what a Christian is, wrong?
Is the Bible declaring Christians no longer have to sin, or is it

declaring Christians no longer sin? The Bible is declaring Christians no longer sin. But I still sin, and I know I'm a Christian. We need to ask ourselves, 'Do we truly believe Scripture?'

Take Romans 6:3-7, especially 6:5,

> For if we have been united with him in a death like his, we will certainly also be united with him in a resurrection like his.

When we become born-again believers with the indwelling of the Holy Spirit, we're told we're united with Christ. If we're united with Christ and Christ is united with us, how can we sin? If we have been crucified with Christ, sin has been crucified in us. Our old self who was a slave to sin has been crucified and killed.

The Christian identity is found in the new creation.

> Therefore, if anyone is in Christ, the new creation has come: The old has gone, the new is here! (2 Corinthians 5:17)

Our new creation pledges its allegiance to God through Christ Jesus.

This is our true identity, we're new creations, united in Christ. Our old Adamic man has been crucified, but we have also been resurrected in Christ. This means we have conquered sin.

Is the Bible suggesting Christians do not sin?

No, it's not suggesting, it's declaring we don't. Let's look at some other Scriptures confirming this.

> So I say, walk by the Spirit, and you will not gratify the desires of the flesh. (Galatians 5:16)

You will not. That's a declaration, not a suggestion.

> We know anyone born of God does not continue to sin; the One who was born of God keeps them safe, and the evil one cannot harm them. (1 John 5:18)

The born-again Christian does not continue to sin.

> No one who is born of God will continue to sin, because God's seed remains in them; they cannot continue sinning, because they have been born of God. (1 John 3:9)

> As obedient children, do not conform to the evil desires you had when you lived in ignorance. But as he who called you is holy, so be holy in all you do; for it is written: 'Be holy, because I am holy.' (1 Peter 1:14-16)

> But if anyone obeys his word, love for God is truly made complete in them. This is how we know we're in him: Whoever claims to live in him must live as Jesus did. (1 John 2:5-6)

As shown earlier, this is probably not our reality, because we continue to sin. So how can these Scriptural statements claim such bold facts that Christians do not sin?

Romans chapter 7 brings the answer to this painful predicament.

This next passage of Scripture has produced provocative debates and no one seems to agree who this 'wretched man' is. I truly believe if we understand who this man is, the rest of Scripture starts to make sense.

This next passage is long, and in order to understand how Scripture can make such bold statements about our position as Christians, we need to view it more closely.

> Was that which is good made death unto me? God forbid. But

sin, that it might appear sin, working death in me by that which is good; that sin by the commandment might become exceeding sinful.

For we know that the law is spiritual: but I am carnal, sold under sin. For that which I do I allow not: for what I would, that do I not; but what I hate, that do I. If I do that which I would not, I consent unto the law that it is good. It is no more I that do it, but sin that dwelleth in me.

For I know that in me (that is, in my flesh,) dwelleth no good thing: for to will is present with me; but how to perform that which is good I find not. For the good that I would I do not: but the evil which I would not, that I do. Now if I do that I would not, it is no more I that do it, but sin that dwelleth in me.

I find a law, that, when I would do good, evil is present with me. For I delight in the law of God after the inward man: But I see another law in my members, warring against the law of my mind, and bringing me into captivity to the law of sin which is in my members.

O wretched man that I am! Who shall deliver me from the body of this death? (Romans 7:13-24 KJV)[4]

Before we establish who this 'wretched man' is, we need to establish who he isn't.

Is he a non-Christian? No.

Romans 3:10-13 says there is no one who understands and there is no one who seeks God, both Jew and Gentile. These verses show a non-Christian working out things in their own strength is blind to the righteous requirements of God's law.

These passages are saying this man has been spiritually awakened.

---

4   Out of all the English versions, the King James Version is the most accurate concerning this passage of Scripture.

For we know that the law is spiritual... (Romans 7:14)

For the good that I would I do not... (Romans 7:19)

For I delight in the law of God after the inward man. (Romans 7:22)

Wherefore the law is holy, and the commandment holy, and just, and good. (Romans 7:12)

This can't be a non-Christian because this understanding and these inward desires to please God have been spiritually awakened.

For I was alive without the law once: but when the commandment came... (Romans 7:9)

God's righteous requirements can only be fully understood when we have been spiritually awakened.
This 'wretched man' has been spiritually awakened and therefore can't be a non-Christian.
Is he a Christian? No.

For sin, taking occasion by the commandment, deceived me, and by it slew me. (Romans 7:11)

If I do that which I would not, I consent unto the law that it is good. (Romans 7:16)

This point needs to be made clear concerning the commandment and the law written about here. These are the righteous commandments or the righteous law God requires and only understood by those who belong to Him.

This is Paul writing about himself and it's generally known Paul was an expert in the Law before he became a Christian. So how can he write about himself in Romans 7:9, 'For I was alive without the law once: but when the commandment came, sin revived, and I died.' How can Paul say, 'For I was alive without the law once…?'

When he obeyed the law before, he obeyed it by man's standard, not God's. For example, if they didn't actually commit adultery, they obeyed the law. But Jesus shone true light on what the commandment required.

> You have heard it was said, 'You shall not commit adultery.' But I tell you anyone who looks at a woman lustfully has already committed adultery with her in his heart. (Matthew 5:27-28)

This is one of the sins Paul had failed in.

> What shall we say? Is the law sin? God forbid. Nay, I had not known sin, but by the law: for I had not known lust, except the law had said, Thou shalt not covet. (Romans 7:7)

Covet here means wrongfully desire. It's the Spirit highlighting the requirements of the law, and it's only through the Spirit can we obey this law.

Getting back to this 'wretched man', the verses within this passage of Romans clearly tell us this isn't a Christian because he is sold under sin, and the Bible clearly tells us we're not sold under sin.

> You have been set free from sin and have become slaves to righteousness. (Romans 6:18)

If this 'wretched man' isn't a non-Christian and he isn't a Christian, what is he?

Within the passages of Romans 7:13-24 the answer is given.

For we know the law is spiritual: but I am carnal, sold under sin. (Romans 7:14)

For I know that in me (that is, in my flesh,) dwelleth no good thing... (Romans 7:18 KJV)

The 'wretched man' is our carnal nature, or our fleshy worldly nature, or our self-operating outside Christ.

The last beast of the heart is the Self.

When we become Christians, we're new creations (2 Corinthians 5:17, Galatians 6:15), born-again (John 3:3, 3:7, 1 Peter 1:23), children of God (John 1:12, Romans 8:14, Galatians 3:26, 1 John 3:1-2, 3:10, 5:2, 5:19). As Christians we're in Christ. We're connected to His death and resurrection. Christians are already victorious because of what Christ has accomplished. Christians no longer sin because of what Christ has accomplished.

The awakening accompanying our choice to receive our Saviour and all He has done places us directly into eternity with Him. We walk with Him 'in this world but not of it'. We walk in His Victory with Him, forever.

Christians still live in a corruptible, perishable body and sin still lies dormant within. This nature of ours is known as the 'carnal nature' or the 'flesh'. It's when we operate in our own strength, not submitted to Christ. When we walk in anything less than His Victory.

Jesus addresses this in Luke 9:23.

> He said to them all: 'Whoever wants to be my disciple must deny themselves and take up their cross daily and follow me.'

Jesus is telling all those who follow Him to put something to death every day. What is Jesus telling us to kill every day? Our carnal fleshy nature.

Why do we need to kill this every day? Because our carnal fleshy nature does not submit to Christ.

How do we kill it? By receiving and keeping our eyes on His Victory, by knowing it isn't about who we are, it's entirely about who He is and, by faith, walking in that simple certainty.

The Bible makes it clear this fleshy carnal nature does not belong to our Christian life.

'There is therefore now no condemnation to them who are in Christ Jesus, who walk not after the flesh, but after the Spirit. For the law of the Spirit of life in Christ Jesus has made me free from the law of sin and death. For what the law was powerless to do because it was weakened by the flesh, God did by sending his own Son in the likeness of sinful flesh to be a sin offering.

And so he condemned sin in the flesh, in order the righteous requirement of the law might be fully met in us, who do not live according to the flesh but according to the Spirit. Those who live according to the flesh have their minds set on what the flesh desires; but those who live in accordance with the Spirit have their minds set on what the Spirit desires. The mind governed by the flesh is death, but the mind governed by the Spirit is life and peace. The mind governed by the flesh is hostile to God; it does not submit to God's law, nor can it do so.

Those who are in the realm of the flesh cannot please God. You, however, are not in the realm of the flesh but are in the realm of the Spirit, if indeed the Spirit of God lives in you. And if anyone does not have the Spirit of Christ, they do not belong to Christ. But if Christ is in you, even though your body is subject to death because of sin, the Spirit gives life because of righteousness. And if the Spirit of him who raised Jesus from the dead is living in you, he who raised Christ from the dead will also give life to your mortal bodies because of his Spirit who lives in you.

Therefore, brothers and sisters, we have an obligation – but it is not to the flesh, to live according to it. For if you live according to the flesh, you will die; but if by the Spirit you put to death the misdeeds of the body, you will live. For those who are led by the Spirit of God are the children of God. The Spirit you received does not make you slaves, so that you live in fear again; rather, the Spirit you received brought about your adoption to sonship. And by him we cry, 'Abba, Father'. (Romans 8:1-15)

Romans 7 tells us what wretched men and women we are when we operate in our carnal fleshy nature.

What a wretched man I am! Who will rescue me from this body that is subject to death? (Romans 7:24)

Thanks be to God, who delivers me through Jesus Christ our Lord. So I myself in my mind am a slave to God's law, but in my sinful nature a slave to the law of sin. (Romans 7:25)

Romans chapter eight tells us how we can truly deal with this carnal fleshy nature.

As Christians, there is a duel battle raging within us until we meet Christ face to face and are transformed from the corruptible to the incorruptible, from the perishable to the imperishable (1 Corinthians 15:52-54).

Until then, as Christians, there will always be warfare of the Spirit against the flesh, because our carnal fleshy nature wars against the Spirit. It's a duel to the death.

This point is important. Our carnal fleshy nature isn't Christian. The Bible emphatically tells us this.

> The mind governed by the flesh is death, but the mind governed by the Spirit is life and peace. The mind governed by the flesh is hostile to God; it does not submit to God's law, nor can it do so. Those who are in the realm of the flesh cannot please God. (Romans 8:6-8)

When we operate in our carnal fleshy nature, we're hostile to God, we can't submit to God's will nor can we do so, and operating in the flesh leads to death.

For all who have accepted Jesus Christ as Lord of their lives, there are two natures within us, our born-again regenerated nature which is Spirit-led and our carnal fleshy nature which gives rise to sin dormant within the members of our body.

With this understanding of this dual battle, all the Scriptures concerning carnal flesh and the Spirit make sense.

We have already seen some examples from Romans, here are some other examples.

> Watch and pray so that you will not fall into temptation. The spirit is willing, but the flesh is weak. (Matthew 26:41)

> So I say, walk by the Spirit, and you will not gratify the desires of the flesh. For the flesh desires what is contrary to the Spirit, and the Spirit what is contrary to the flesh. (Galatians 5:16-17)

They are in conflict with each other, so that you are not to do whatever you want.

Those who belong to Christ Jesus have crucified the flesh with its passions and desires. Since we live by the Spirit, let us keep in step with the Spirit. (Galatians 5:24-25)

The Apostle Paul recognised this conflict and wrote about it often.

> Do you not know that in a race all the runners run, but only one gets the prize? Run in such a way as to get the prize. Everyone who competes in the games goes into strict training. They do it to get a crown that will not last, but we do it to get a crown that will last forever.
>
> Therefore I do not run like someone running aimlessly; I do not fight like a boxer beating the air. No, I strike a blow to my body and make it my slave so that after I have preached to others, I myself will not be disqualified for the prize. (1 Corinthians 9:24-27)

Paul knew this battle, he tried to fight it in his own strength and failed miserably. He did learn it's already won in Christ Jesus and walking in the Spirit is the only answer. We must put the flesh to death.

What a predicament. We can't live sinless perfect lives; that's guaranteed to fail. We need to know the reality of what we face within ourselves.

As Christians, there are two paths we can choose, the Spiritual or the carnal. The harsh reality is if we're not continually pursuing Christ, our carnal nature will prevail.

That's why Jesus said, 'Take up your cross daily and follow me.'

Chapter 17

Our Identity Struggle

Our identity rests with our true and false identities concerning the flesh and the Spirit.

Identity is one of our most important markers in deciding which direction we walk. Our true identity is wrapped up in God, and He gave us our identity right at the beginning.

> God said, 'Let us make mankind in our image, in our likeness, so that they may rule over the fish in the sea and the birds in the sky, over the livestock and all the wild animals, and over all the creatures that move along the ground.'
>
> God created mankind in his own image, in the image of God he created them; male and female he created them. (Genesis 1:26-27)

> The LORD God formed a man from the dust of the ground and breathed into his nostrils the breath of life, and the man became a living being. (Genesis 2:7)

> God saw all that he had made, and it was very good. And there was evening, and there was morning – the sixth day. (Genesis 1:31)

This was our true identity with no barriers between us and God. When this relationship between us and God is unhindered, our identity is secure, not insecure. We live in Alpha and Omega, without beginning and without end.

But it didn't take long for this identity to be robbed from us. Our 'likeness to God' is in our ability to choose. The power released in the ability to choose is phenomenal. Man is the only creature with that ability. God gave us that ability because His love for us is perfect. A perfect love must allow the right of refusal.

We exercised that ability to choose in direct defiance of our Maker, and our identity crisis started right there, in the Garden of Eden.

Not before God first warned man.

> And the LORD God commanded the man, 'You are free to eat from any tree in the garden; but you must not eat from the tree of the knowledge of good and evil, for when you eat from it you will certainly die.' (Genesis 2:16-17)

The historical story of Eve and the forbidden fruit is well documented, but there is a verse we need to look at that promised much but delivered a lie. The Devil, speaking through the serpent, deceived Eve.

> 'You will not certainly die,' the serpent said to the woman. 'For God knows that when you eat from it your eyes will be opened, and you will be like God, knowing good and evil.' (Genesis 3:4-5)

The Devil promised this fruit would enlighten them to unlimited understanding and become like God. The temptation was too great for Eve, who was deceived, and for Adam, who knew better.

It's here our identity was taken away from us and replaced with a false identity. This is where we rejected His uncreated realm, without limitations, where our spirit belongs reconciled with His Spirit for eternity, and chose a created realm we thought we could control.

It looked like a good deal. It wasn't.

This identity drives us away from God rather than toward Him.

> The fool says in his heart, 'There is no God.' They are corrupt, their deeds are vile; there is no one who does good. The LORD looks down from heaven on all mankind to see if there are any who understand, any who seek God. All have turned away, all have become corrupt; there is no one who does good, not even one. (Psalm 14:1-4)

The problem with this false identity is, mankind has fully accepted it and lives comfortably with it.

It's only through faith in obedience to God, can we come out of this false identity.

> For God so loved the world that he gave his one and only Son, that whoever believes in him shall not perish but have eternal life. (John 3:16)

Our true identity is found in the Lord Jesus Christ, the Way, the Truth and the Life. Imagine a horse, trapped in a two-acre paddock forever, and a horse running free down an endless beach. The spirit of man, through Christ, is intended by God to be the horse running free in eternity, not trapped in a limited, constricted realm of unfulfilled carnal appetites.

As Christians, we should be operating in this true identity, but reality proves otherwise. When we walk in the Spirit and are operating under the Lordship of Christ Jesus, we're experiencing our true identity.

When we believe the Word of God about us and allow that to be applied to our lives, this is who we truly are.

But there is a problem, our old identity still believes it has a right to our lives.

We will struggle with our old false identity for the rest of our lives on this earth, that's why Jesus said we must put it death (Luke 9:23-24).

> Do not conform to the pattern of this world, but be transformed by the renewing of your mind. (Romans 12:2)

Our old identity belongs to the world's pattern and it's something that will not go away easily. The struggle found in Romans 7:14-24 is part of this old identity, but it's more than the obvious wrongs.

When we fall back onto our old identity, we're operating in our own strength, wisdom and knowledge. This will seem Godly and can deceive us into believing we're walking in the Spirit.

But this old identity will never submit to Christ because it's of the Tree of Knowledge. No matter how righteous it may look, it does not surrender to Jesus.

We will always struggle with our old identity and the more we fight against it, the more determined it seems to become, as it says in Romans 7:20-24,

> If I do what I do not want of do, it is no longer I who do it, but it is sin living in me that does it. So I find this law at work.
>
> Although I want to do good, evil is right there with me. For in my inner being I delight in God's law, but I see another law at work in me, waging war against the law of my mind and making me a prisoner of the law of sin at work within me. What a wretched man I am! Who will rescue me from this body that is subject to death?

Our Identity Struggle

We must learn to recognise our true and false identities deal with them appropriately. The answer is in Romans 7:25,

> Thanks be to God, who delivers me through Jesus Christ our Lord! So I myself in my mind am a slave to God's law, but in my sinful nature (false identity) a slave to the law of sin.

Our old false identity is our default position. We have to be vigilant in keeping our hearts and eyes fixed on the Lord Jesus Christ.

Chapter 18

Mediocrity

One of the main characteristics of a Two Talent Servant is mediocrity. This is a comfortable place to be for Christians because it offers no real sacrifice and a place in the Kingdom is still guaranteed.

The problem with this position is usually we don't realise we're in it. We like to think we have a good relationship with Christ and certain things keep side-tracking us.

For many years this was the state I was in. I knew in my heart Christ still dwelt in my life, but for a big part, I seemed to be drifting. There were periods of Spiritual spurts, but they never remained consistent.

Nothing in the world could entice me away from Christ, but I still let the influence of the world, have room to move. One thing I did know, I knew I wasn't where God really wanted me.

Mediocrity is when we know we're servants of the Most High God and we're not acting like servants of the Most High God. When we know in our hearts we're not as committed as we would like to be, when our spirit is willing, but our flesh is weak.

We make excuses for our habitual sins and lack of discipline. We tend to blame everything and everyone else except ourselves. Whatever the reason, we know we're not fully submitted to Christ.

Before we see how the Bible addresses this problem, let us look at how mediocrity affects us approaching the things of God. The

Bible has always needed the Holy Spirit to understand it correctly. The problem with mediocrity is we're not always under the influence of the Holy Spirit.

When we allow the flesh to live, a major part of us doesn't want to read the Bible and we obey that part. And even when we do read the Word, we may be reading it in our own strength and understanding, bringing no real change.

When Scripture is truly understood, it's addressing full surrender.

As mediocre believers, a lot of Scripture we read does not apply to us. When we read passages concerning fully surrendered believers, it's an ideal, not a reality. Or we read it without it truly sinking in and miss the deeper requirement of the passage.

Scripture helps keep the mediocre Christians alive, but not all benefits of Scripture can be applied to them. Mediocrity will subtly hinder us in the full benefit of Scriptural reading.

Prayer life, or communicating with God, is the one that most notably suffers. Mediocrity can't come boldly before the Throne room, because we tend to shy away from God when we know we're slacking.

When we do sincerely pray, it's either in a crisis or when we really want something. Communication between Christ Jesus and ourselves becomes distant, because when we're operating in the flesh, the flesh is an enemy to Christ.

> The mind governed by the flesh is hostile to God; it does not submit to God's law, nor can it do so. Those who are in the realm of the flesh cannot please God. Therefore, brothers and sisters, we have an obligation – but it isn't to the flesh, to live according to it. (Romans 8:7-8, 12)

Prayer is faith-driven communication between you and God. Mediocrity can bring doubt and uncertainty. There is a part of us wanting to believe and a part of us that's not so sure, leaving room for the part that wants to outright rebel.

Our faith can be tainted, making our prayers less effective. The Amplified Version best describes what prayer should be in James 5:16b,

> ...the earnest (heartfelt, continued) prayer of a righteous man makes tremendous power available [dynamic in its working].

Can mediocrity rise up to this level on a consistent basis?

Fellowship with other believers is also affected. Mediocrity will tend to cause us to shy away from them or get us to communicate at a less demanding level. Our conversations may have Christ Jesus involved, but there will be no real conviction behind what we say, because we're not fully surrendered to what we believe.

The Bible says how we're to function:

> ...so that there should be no division in the body, but that its parts should have equal concern for each other. If one part suffers, every part suffers with it; if one part is honoured every part rejoices with it. Now you are the body of Christ, and each one of you is a part of it. (1 Corinthians 12:25-27)

We're to be unified and in one Spirit, edifying and encouraging one another. Being part of Christ's body means we're operating the way he wants us to operate. This is crucial for the body of believers. Individual, flesh-driven wills can seldom find unity. In Christ's body that union is intrinsic.

This is only truly possible when we're walking in the Spirit and not the flesh. Mediocrity makes parts of the body non-functional, or functional at less than its optimum capacity.

There are many more areas that are affected, but let's look at how to counter this.

The best person to understand where you stand with God is you. There may be a feeling of dissatisfaction concerning a really meaningful, consistent relationship with Christ. You sense you are missing God's mark, more often than not.

There is a desire to do better, but it never seems to get off the ground. You know you're not putting the effort in, allowing many things to crowd Jesus Christ out.

Rejoice.

If you're dissatisfied with where you are with Christ, rejoice. It's most likely the Holy Spirit making you feel this way. The Spirit knows what it takes to have a meaningful life and it isn't about what we can accomplish in this world. It's about the relationship we have with the Lord Jesus Christ.

Only when we decide to die to our excuses and distractions and make Christ Jesus the priority we pursue can we seriously start to conquer mediocrity.

Chapter 19

A Milk Diet

> In fact, though by this time you ought to be teachers, you need someone to teach you the elementary truths of God's word all over again. You need milk, not solid food! Anyone who lives on milk, being still an infant, is not acquainted with the teaching about righteousness. But solid food is for the mature, who by constant use have trained themselves to distinguish good from evil. (Hebrews 5:12-14)

There has been a misconception among Christians equating eating meat to understanding the meatier parts of Scripture. But the verses above all tell us those on a milk diet don't have the ability to reach these deeper levels of understanding with the Lord.

Here we have a concept that seems straightforward, but realistically, it's difficult. To walk obediently before Christ.

> Jesus replied, 'Anyone who loves me will obey my teaching. My Father will love them, and we will come to them and make our home with them.' (John 14:23)

The key to advancing beyond the milk stage to meat eaters, or from the immature to the mature concerning righteousness, is Hebrews 5:14,

> But solid food is for the mature, who by constant use have trained themselves to distinguish good from evil.

There are three factors needing looking at. Perseverance, persistence and perception.

This process runs throughout Scripture and is one of the fundamental keys to maturity. Righteousness is one of the requirements for a successful Christian life and it can't be human righteousness, but God's Righteousness. One of the ways to gain this Righteousness is through obedience.

To understand what God requires of us, to be righteous, we need to understand what Righteousness is.

Righteousness isn't the virtuous good we produce, or even the good we produce as Christians. Righteousness is mostly perceived through actions. It's not man-made, and it's not in our actions. Righteousness is God the Father, God the Son and God the Holy Spirit.

When we submit to the Lord Jesus Christ and do His will, this is righteousness. When we walk in this obedience, it allows the Father and Son's presence to reside and work through us.

When we persevere and persist in this, we will perceive what is good and evil, knowing what is of God and what isn't.

How do we achieve this? Perseverance is a key factor. This stops us from giving up and it gives us tangible experiences to make us realise we can succeed in Christ.

We'll face many situations giving us the opportunity to obey Christ's teaching or not. Walking obediently before God is both simple and difficult.

It's simple because there are many things we know that are not from God and we know participating in them doesn't please Him. The difficulty is these things can be habits we tend to slip into, or draw us in like a powerful magnet.

If we allow these habitual sins to remain in our lives, it will affect us, whether knowingly, or unknowingly.

We have to choose whether we want to obey Christ or not. Obedience unlocks the ability to overcome.

Learning to surrender to what Christ wants rather than giving into our fleshy desires or responses, is what puts our feet on firm foundations. When we surrender to Christ, we experience His strength to do what's right.

> Therefore, since we're surrounded by such a great cloud of witnesses, let us throw off everything that hinders and the sin that so easily entangles. And let us run with perseverance the race marked out for us, fixing our eyes on Jesus, the pioneer and perfecter of faith. For the joy set before him he endured the cross, scorning its shame, and sat down at the right hand of the throne of God. (Hebrews 12:1-2)

The bad habits, strong temptations, responding wrongly, all the things our carnal nature so easily entangles itself with, need no longer be a stumbling block. When we fix our eyes on Christ, He gives us His abilities.

When we learn to respond in the Spirit and not the flesh, we must persevere. These challenges will not disappear. They will arise again and again, and perseverance is the key to growing from strength to strength.

Walking continually in obedience not only makes our foundations (in Christ) firm, but it allows God to reveal more of Himself to us.

> LORD, who may dwell in your sacred tent? Who may live on your holy mountain? The ones whose walk is blameless, who do what is righteous, who speak the truth from their heart; whose

> tongues utters no slander, who do no wrong to a neighbour, and cast no slur on others, who despise a vile person but honour those who fear the LORD; who keep an oath even when it hurts, and do not change their mind; who lend money to the poor without interest; who do not accept a bribe against the innocent. Whoever does these things will never be shaken. (Psalm 15:1-5)

Choosing to walk obediently with Christ again and again is exactly what Scripture encourages us to do. This is the training ground for discernment concerning what is of God and what isn't.

Perseverance and persistence will bring the right perception. Continual obedience brings us into God's understanding, we're able to see things more clearly. We're able to distinguish between good and evil.

> Therefore, I urge you, brothers and sisters, in view of God's mercy, to offer your bodies as a living sacrifice, holy and pleasing to God – this is your true and proper worship.
>
> Do not conform to the pattern of this world, but be transformed by the renewing of your mind. You will be able to test and approve what God's will is – his good, pleasing and perfect will. (Romans 12:1-2)

A meat-eating Christian isn't someone who can confidently interpret Scripture, but someone who consistently chooses to do what is right before the eyes of God.

Chapter 20

Eyes on Man

Before we get into the dangers of wrong concepts of leadership, we need to understand good leadership is a necessary part of the church.

It's good to be accountable to our Spiritual leadership, which in turn, should be in step with Christ Jesus. It's wise to be accountable to spiritual leadership; this is biblical when done correctly.

> Brothers and sisters, I could not address you as people who live by the Spirit but as people who are still worldly – mere infants in Christ. I gave you milk, not solid food, for you were not ready for it.
>
> Indeed, you are still not ready. You are still worldly. For since there is jealousy and quarrelling among you, are you not worldly? Are you not acting like mere humans? For when one says, 'I follow Paul,' and another, 'I follow Apollos,' are you not mere human beings? (1 Corinthians 3-4)

John the Baptist spoke these words in John 3:31,

> The one who comes from above is above all; the one who is from the earth belongs to the earth, and speaks as one from the earth. The one who comes from heaven is above all.

John the Baptist was talking about how Jesus was greater because He was from heaven and we're from this earth. We will more naturally follow the pattern of this world rather than God's way.

Members of the church in Corinth fell into this trap. Their eyes were on their leaders and not on Christ, and they were even comparing their leaders with each other.

There is nothing wrong with church leadership, the Bible certainly advocates this. It's when leadership becomes the head, instead of Christ, it becomes a problem.

The church is the body and the Lord Jesus Christ is the head. Church leadership encourages the members of the body to look to Christ and fellowship in unity. The leadership is still part of the body and must be submitted to the head, which is the Lord Jesus Christ.

> And he is the head of the body, the church; he is the beginning and the firstborn from among the dead, so in everything he might have the supremacy. For God was pleased to have all his fullness dwell in him. (Colossians 1:18-19)

When we take our eyes off Christ and start to put them on people around us the dangers can start to creep in. There are many dangers arising from this, but we will look at two.

When we place one particular person higher than everyone else that person becomes the mediator between you and God. Our moral compass can be tied up in this person.

When we give responsibility over to them we look toward the leadership as the head and not Christ Jesus.

Paul was angry at this because the eyes of the people had been lowered to a human level. When our standards have been lowered to this level, the level of spiritual maturity is lowered. There are many subtle factors playing out in this scenario.

We place the leadership higher than ourselves spiritually. This can falsely give the impression the leader has got it together and we haven't, putting us in a continual state of dependency on that leader.

We can perceive the leadership doesn't have the same weaknesses, they don't keep falling to sin, they seem to be more successful. They must have the answer for our problems.

But because other humans can't truly change our sinful nature, these problems never seem to go away.

True leadership should always point us to Jesus Christ, making us more dependent on God than man or woman.

We can project our responsibility for morality onto them. A good example is a fanatical sports fan. A sports fan wants their sportsperson or team to win and leaves all the necessary preparations to them. There is no requirement on their behalf to be as disciplined as their team or sportsperson.

When we have projected the spiritual leadership within our lives to a higher level than ourselves, we can believe it's important for them to be spiritually mature and not as important for ourselves.

We have in some way projected our moral responsibility onto them, putting us in the stands rather than on the field of play.

Elevating our leadership in an unhealthy manner can also leave us less accountable. When we look toward the leaders for our moral accountability, we're setting them up to be exactly like false gods and idols the pagans worship.

The reason false gods and idols don't work is because they only have an external and limited influence on us.

We want to be good on their behalf, but they're blind to what we're thinking, feeling and even experiencing.

It leaves us with large gaps in our reality which are not accountable to them, which in turn, leaves us vulnerable.

Elevating our leadership in the wrong light can leave us with weak foundations. Because our eyes are fixed on the leadership rather than Christ, our soundness is built on their foundations.

When they are taken away from us or even fall because of sin, our world can come crashing around us.

We must respect our leadership, but they must never become the head, that role is only reserved for the Lord Jesus Christ. Christ must be the foundation we rely on. If our eyes are fixed on Christ, we will recognise Godly leadership concerning His will for our lives.

We will have a healthy relationship respecting the leadership placed over us, but Christ remains the foundation we're built on.

Our perspective of leadership must be correct where Jesus Christ remains the head and we alongside our leadership, are submitting to the Lord.

Secondly; the body without the head. This horrified Paul because he knew first-hand what it meant to have men lead the way, instead of God.

The religious rulers, including the Pharisees of which he was one, took it upon themselves to herald the truth. Unfortunately, their truth was from the perspective of man, not God. This is how bad it had become in Jesus' day.

> Woe to you, teachers of the law and Pharisees, you hypocrites. You shut the door of the kingdom of heaven in people's faces. You yourselves do not enter, nor will you let those enter who are trying to.
>
> Woe to you, teachers of the law and Pharisees, you hypocrites.
>
> You travel over land and sea to win a single convert and when you have succeeded, you make them twice as much a child of hell as you are.
>
> Woe to you, teachers of the law and Pharisees, you hypocrites. You give a tenth of your spices – mint, dill and cumin. But you have neglected the more important matters of the law – justice,

mercy and faithfulness. You should have practised the latter, without neglecting the former.

Woe to you, teachers of the law and Pharisees, you hypocrites. You clean the outside of the cup and dish, but inside they are full of greed and self-indulgence.

Woe to you, teachers of the law and Pharisees, you hypocrites. You are like whitewashed tombs, beautiful on the outside but on the inside full of the bones of the dead and everything unclean. (Matthew 23:13, 15, 23, 25, 27)

When a group of people or a church is operating as the heralds of truth, but are not actually submitted or receiving Ruach truth from Jesus Christ, that truth will always be earth-formed and not Heaven sent.

Paul knew the dire consequences when man is the driving force rather than God. Jesus Christ must always remain the head of the body or church, if not, that church will always, without exception, drift away from the Truth.

How do you know if Jesus Christ is the head of the church?

The Lord Jesus is revered and honoured through all spheres of the church. His will is priority and believing and obeying His commands takes precedence.

Jesus replied, 'Anyone who loves me will obey my teaching. My Father will love them, and we will come to them and make our home with them.

'Anyone who does not love me will not obey my teaching. These words you hear are not my own; they belong to the Father who sent me.' (John 14:23-24)

Chapter 21

Moving On

As Christians, being a Two Talent Servant is probably the easiest path to take. But the problem with this path is it still has parts of the world attached to it. Yes, Jesus Christ is Lord, but He isn't Lord of all. Our spirit is willing, but we still allow the flesh to override this.

Being a Two Talent Servant can even feel comfortable, but being comfortable usually involves lying down or sitting in a snug chair, motionless. When we're in this state, our spiritual growth will usually come to a standstill. We can be stuck at a certain point of our spiritual growth if we're unwilling to move forward.

Two Talent Servants will make it to heaven, but will regret the foolish decisions along the path leading there. Once we go to meet our Saviour, there is no going back.

All the times we decided to walk in the flesh rather than the Spirit, we can't go back and change. All the times when we chose to do it our way, rather than submit to the prompting of the Holy Spirit, those opportunities will be gone.

When we come into the final judgement (1 Corinthians 3:11-15), many of our buildings will be made of flammable material.

But the great news is, if we're still breathing, we can change.

Repentance will give us a clean slate, but our actions must fall into line. If we're willing, God is capable of giving us the ability to become Five Talent Servants.

PART 4

The Five Talent Servant

Chapter 22

Introducing the Five Talent Servant

The great saints before us can be inspiring and intimidating.

Abraham, Moses, Ruth, Esther, Samuel, David, the Prophets, John the Baptist, the Apostle Paul and many others can seem to be out of our league because of what they accomplished for the Lord.

When saints are believing and obeying the Lord, this is what it is to be a Five Talent Servant.

I knew I could never measure up to the super saints. I never imagined I could reach those lofty heights.

I would read verses likes 1 Peter 1:15-16,

> But as he who called you is holy, so be holy in all you do; for it is written: 'Be holy, because I am holy.'

and know exactly what I was like and know I could never measure up to that standard.

Besides that, I had a hard time believing 2 Corinthians 5:17,

> Therefore, if anyone is in Christ, the new creation has come: The old has gone, the new is here.

I always felt I missed the bus when it came to this verse. Again, the old wasn't gone.

To live a life like the heroes of the Faith seemed out of my reach. The biblical fact is, God doesn't want anything less.

When we read the Bible carefully, the One Talent Servants (those who reject Christ) are condemned, the Two Talent Servants are rebuked and disciplined, and the Five Talent Servants are commended.

The Bible is always steering us in this direction and Scripture is more deeply understood by those who truly bear the cross.

When I tried to be a better Christian, or when I was determined not to give in to my weaknesses, it all ended in failure. The reason I failed was because it was me trying. I didn't understand how God wanted me to do it. He isn't asking us to try harder, He wants us to trust Him.

When God started to take me out of the Two Talent realm, He showed me something really important. One of the Scriptures I struggled with was the 'be holy' one. When I thought of myself as being holy, and all that came with that statement, there was no way I thought I could attain it.

It was a simple Bible story shifting my way of thinking about this dilemma. It was the story of Moses and the burning bush bringing the paradigm shift.

> Now Moses was tending the flock of Jethro his father-in-law, the priest of Midian, and he led the flock to the far side of the wilderness and came to Horeb, the mountain of God. There the angel of the LORD appeared to him in flames of fire from within a bush. Moses saw that though the bush was on fire it didn't burn up.
>
> Moses thought, 'I will go over and see this strange sight – why the bush does not burn up.' When the LORD saw that he had gone over to look, God called to him from within the bush,

'Moses! Moses!' And Moses said, 'Here I am.'

'Do not come any closer,' God said. 'Take off your sandals, for the place where you are standing is holy ground.' (Exodus 3:1-5)

What God showed me here completely changed my perspective of holiness.

What made the ground holy? Was it the bush? The flames? The ground? The mountain? The angel, perhaps?

It was the Presence of God. It has nothing to do with us being holy. It's the presence of God making us holy. Wherever the Presence of God is, that place is holy.

This Presence isn't God's omnipresence covering the universe and beyond. Nor is it some casual encounter, or a general covering of God toward all believers. This is the manifest Presence of God, the united in Christ, the illumination of the Holy Spirit.

It's when we're submitted under the authority of the Lord Jesus Christ, when we're walking in the Spirit and not the flesh.

This is what a Five Talent Servant is, someone who has decided to submit to Jesus Christ, rather than themselves or anything else.

The journey of the Five Talent Servant isn't trying to become perfect, it's resting in the arms of the One who is perfect.

It isn't trying to become holy, but choosing to abide in the Presence of the Holy One.

It isn't trying to improve our character but allowing the character of Christ to improve us. It's about taking our eyes off ourselves and what's around us and fixing them on the Lord Jesus Christ. Choosing to walk in the Spirit and not the flesh or carnal nature.

It's submitting to the Lordship of Christ Jesus, taking up the cross daily and dying to our sinful nature. It's staying in communion with God and walking in the realms of His Will, not ours.

The Five Talent Servant is what Jesus' life on this earth was and it's all those who walk as He walked.

If anyone obeys his word, love for God is truly made complete in them. This is how we know we're in him: Whoever claims to live in him must live as Jesus did. (1 John 2:5-6)

CHAPTER 23

Who are Five Talent Servants?

Five Talent Servants have decided to take Luke 9:23-24 seriously.

> He said to them all: 'Whoever wants to be my disciple must deny themselves and take up their cross daily and follow me. For whoever wants to save their life will lose it, but whoever loses their life for me will save it.'

These are Christians whose hearts yearn after the Lord.

> How lovely is your dwelling place, LORD Almighty! My soul yearns, even faints, for the courts of the LORD; my heart and my flesh cry out for the living God. (Psalm 84:1-2)

These are Christians who believe and obey.

> Jesus replied, 'Anyone who loves me will obey my teaching. My Father will love them, and we will come to them and make our home with them.' (John 14:23)

These are Christians who choose to walk in the Spirit and not the flesh.

> The Spirit gives life; the flesh counts for nothing. The words I have spoken to you – they are full of the Spirit and life. (John 6:63)

> The mind governed by the flesh is death, but the mind governed by the Spirit is life and peace. (Romans 8:6)

These are Christians who endure because their eyes are fixed on Christ.

> Therefore we do not lose heart. Though outwardly we're wasting away, yet inwardly we're being renewed day by day. For our light and momentary troubles are achieving for us an eternal glory that far outweighs them all.
> So we fix our eyes not on what is seen, but on what is unseen, since what is seen is temporary, but what is unseen is eternal. (2 Corinthians 4:16-18)

These are Christians who have learnt to trust God.

> Trust in the LORD with all your heart and lean not on your own understanding; in all your ways submit to him, and he will make your paths straight. (Proverbs 3:5-6)

These are Christians who love and obey His Word.

> Blessed are those whose ways are blameless, who walk according to the law of the LORD. Blessed are those who keep his statutes and seek him with all their heart – they do no wrong but follow his ways. (Psalm 119:1-3)

These are Christians who are willing to endure suffering and tribulation for the sake of Christ.

In all this you greatly rejoice, though for a little while you may have had to suffer grief in all kinds of trials.

These have come so the proven genuineness of your faith – of greater worth than gold, which perishes even though refined by fire – may result in praise, glory and honour when Jesus Christ is revealed. (1 Peter 1:6-7)

Five Talent Servants are those who have submitted to the Lordship of Christ Jesus and are willing to lay down their lives for Him. They are not 'super saints', neither are they the most talented among us.

They are the ordinary who choose to believe and obey an extraordinary God.

CHAPTER 24

True Repentance

I recently grappled with a sin relentlessly hounding me for over forty years.

Even though I was able to overcome this sin through the power of Jesus Christ over the years, God needed to do something deeper within me I was unaware of, finally setting me free from the subtle nagging of it.

The sin of lust is a common struggle for Christian men and unfortunately not all are able to break free from it. From about the age of 12, this sin lodged itself into my soul and it became a stronghold.

At the age of 21, I became a Christian and my allegiance changed from a selfish one, to wanting to honour the Lord Jesus Christ.

This sin continued to hound me. There were victories and there were defeats. This sin was buried deep in my soul and only God (and maybe His spiritual enemy) could see it.

In 1992 I married Selina, my beautiful, wonderful wife. This is when I tried really hard to overcome this sin. I truly wanted this sin out of my life, for some reason it wouldn't leave me alone.

And there was a legitimate reason it was still able to hang around, that key would come many years later. God knew what needed to happen, nevertheless, He faithfully continued to reduce the influence it had on me.

In 1997 the Holy Spirit spoke two words, 'Press in.'

This started the journey of a deeper relationship with Christ. It was here where I truly experienced the power of Jesus Christ that gave me the ability to overcome this sin. Even though I knew victory through the power of Christ, the lure of this sin never went away.

This meant I had to remain vigilant and submissive to Christ, because I always felt it hung around probing for a weak spot. Even though my walk with Christ had become more deeply committed, the lure of this sin never went away.

I naturally thought this was a struggle I would have to face for the rest of my life, with the help of Christ, I could become victorious.

God knew what really needed to happen and what was still buried there.

In 1997 when I truly started to pursue Christ I thought the sin of lust was finally being dealt with. What I didn't realise was I never truly repented. I didn't despise or hate this sin and because of this, the root was able to remain beneath the surface.

The tree and the fruits of that tree were removed, the root remained. This sin lay dormant within me waiting for the opportunity to spring to life.

The root affected me more than I realised. I was unaware of how it affected my wife. For some reason agitation would regularly visit our marriage. Because I had not dealt with this sin thoroughly, the agitation made for an often volatile marriage.

Only God's grace and His secure hands have protected this marriage.

God takes the order of authority seriously. As the husband and father, sins and even dormant roots of sin have more effect than we realise. Men need to take the role seriously and with sober understanding.

It was the effect on my wife that finally enabled me to confront this sin.

God's refining fire drew up some unpleasant sins I had buried deep in my soul. My wife was able to fish them out. She became the key to finally dealing with this lodged root. The hurt it was causing her made me, for the first time in my life, really hate and despise this sin.

I came before God stripped of all pretence and repented from the depth of my heart. I wanted every part of this sin out of my life. Transparency with my wife and a Christian couple we hold ourselves accountable to was the path to finally set me completely free from this sinful root.

I felt this sin was living in my basement, even though through the power of Christ Jesus, I didn't have to feed it, it was still in my basement.

When I truly repented, God was able to rip this root out of my life and my house no longer has that sin lingering in the basement. My intrinsic nature means I have to remain vigilant, having that root removed has made a huge difference.

God's desire for us is to be set free from the influence of sin. We must come to a place of genuine honesty concerning lingering sins refusing to leave us alone.

They linger because we do not hate and despise them, or we make excuses and justify why we respond in a certain way.

When we truly repent, standing completely and honestly before God, He is able to remove roots we may not even be aware of.

When we experience true freedom we can appreciate Romans 12:1-2,

> Therefore, I urge you, brothers and sisters, in view of God's mercy, to offer your bodies as a living sacrifice, holy and pleasing to God – this is your true and proper worship.

Do not conform to the pattern of this world, be transformed by the renewing of your mind. You will be able to test and approve what God's will is – his good, pleasing and perfect will.

Chapter 25

United in Christ

> We were therefore buried with him through baptism into death in order that, as Christ was raised from the dead through the glory of the Father, we too may live a new life.
> For if we have been united with him in death like his, we will certainly be united with him in a resurrection like his. (Romans 6:4-5)

Understanding this Scripture is truly mind-blowing, because there are two massive truths happening here.

First, 'buried with him'. This, when fully understood by believers, is truly transforming. When Christ Jesus died on the cross, every aspect of sin was put to death there. This includes the sin affecting us as Christians today.

Our sinful nature died on the cross with Christ.

> For we know our old self was crucified with him so the body ruled by sin might be done away with, that we should no longer be slaves to sin – because anyone who has died has been set free from sin. (Romans 6:6-7)

When Christ died on the cross, He took our sinful nature and put it to death. We're no longer subject to sin. That part of us died with Christ on the cross.

Five Talent Servants understand what it is to be united in his death. This truly transforms the way they think about sin.

Watchmen Nee, in his book *The Path of Progress*, in a chapter titled 'Reckoning', explains this wonderfully. This is what he said when the revelation of what this meant hit him. 'I was carried away with such joy at this great discovery I jumped up from my chair and cried, "Praise the Lord, I am dead!"'

What Watchmen Nee understood was he was already dead in Christ. He knew he died with Christ on the cross. This was significant because it dealt with the struggle with sin correctly. He wrote, 'From that day to this I have never for one moment doubted the finality of that word: "I have been crucified with Christ."'

It's to be taken as fact and we're to understand it as true.

> The death he died, he died to sin once for all; the life he lives, he lives to God. In the same way, count yourselves dead to sin but alive to God in Christ Jesus. (Romans 6:10-11)

When Christ died on the cross, sin died with Him. If we're united in Christ, our sin died with Him. We no longer try to not sin, we submit to Christ, because our sin has already been conquered. When we truly unite with Christ, how can we sin?

Paul writes about this in Philippians 3:10-11,

> I want to know Christ – yes, to know the power of his resurrection and participation in his sufferings, becoming like him in his death, and so, somehow, attaining to the resurrection from the dead.

This statement from Paul was referring to his old fleshy carnal life celebrating his self-righteousness, Christ's death sets him free from this.

We have a choice, because we battle with the two natures within us, the new creation in Christ and the carnal nature. When we submit to Christ Jesus, sin is dead to us.

We truly become what Jesus told us in Luke 9:23,

> He said to them all: 'Whoever wants to be my disciple must deny themselves and take up their cross daily and follow me.'

The Bible never promises this would be easy, we may have to suffer, the Holy Spirit will give us the ability.

> It is God who makes both us and you stand firm in Christ. He anointed us. (2 Corinthians 1:21)

This is the position God wants us to have and through Jesus Christ, He can empathise with us concerning temptation.

> For we do not have a high priest who is unable to empathise with our weaknesses, we have one who has been tempted in every way, as we're – yet he did not sin.
> Let us approach God's throne of grace with confidence, so we may receive mercy and find grace to help us in our time of need. (Hebrews 4:15-16)

It isn't us trying to conquer sin, it's us submitting to Christ Jesus through the Spirit, because He has conquered sin.

It's understanding we have already died with Christ and we're no longer slaves to sin, and slaves to righteousness.

Because we have the Holy Spirit, we have the choice whether we're going to submit to Christ Jesus or our flesh. God never takes the ability to choose away, He continually gives us the opportunity for victory in Him.

The hardest part of temptation for us isn't the temptation, it's whether we want to submit to Christ. Once submitted, it's His Spirit lifting us beyond the sin. Sin never gives up easily, it may hang around. Christ gives us the power to refuse it entry.

Uniting with Christ is being resurrected with Him. The fulfilment of this will only occur when we meet Jesus with our incorruptible bodies, when we die or get caught up with Him upon His return. Paul hints at experiencing a portion of this while we're still here.

> I want to know Christ – yes, to know the power of his resurrection and participation in his sufferings, becoming like him in his death, and so, somehow, attaining to the resurrection from the dead.
>
> Not that I have already obtained all this, or have already arrived at my goal, I press on to take hold of that for which Christ Jesus took hold of me. (Philippians 3:10-12)

Here we see Paul acknowledging we will not attain the fullness of this while on this earth, yet we can experience it by dying to our carnal nature and submitting to Jesus Christ.

Paul so hungered for this to be a part of his life, he described his former life as 'dung' (Philippians 3:8)[5] compared with the life he can have in Christ Jesus.

This is all great, but what does it mean to be united in His resurrection?

---

5 'Yea doubtless, and I count all things but loss for the excellency of the knowledge of Christ Jesus my Lord: for whom I have suffered the loss of all things, and do count them but *dung*, that I may win Christ.' (KJV)

As Christians we're united with Him, we join in that resurrection. The example of baptism illustrates this. The watery grave represents our new life in Christ, from the dying of the old self, to being resurrected in our new nature.

Whenever we're operating as new creations walking in the Spirit, submitted to Jesus Christ, we're living resurrected lives. As Jesus said, we must take up the cross daily, which means every day we're dying to our fleshy carnal nature and following Christ.

The resurrected life is walking with Christ. It may not be exciting or on fire all the time. Walking in the Spirit means having the manifest Presence of God enabling us with His peace, joy and wisdom.

Chapter 26

United in His Suffering

Why does the Bible celebrate suffering, trials and tribulations?

> Not only so, but we glory in our sufferings, because we know suffering produces perseverance; perseverance, character, and character, hope. (Romans 5:3-4)

> Consider it pure joy, my brothers and sisters, whenever you face trials of many kinds, because you know the testing of your faith produces perseverance. Let perseverance finish its work so you may be mature and complete, not lacking anything. (James 1:2-4)

Instead of focusing on how to get through these trials, this section of the book focusses on why they are necessary.

Romans 5:3-4 describes the process of sanctification or being moulded by the hand of God. And the first product is perseverance, mentioned in James 1:2-4.

Why is perseverance important?

Because we serve a God of reality. God knows we live in a fallen world and we reside in a body that is still corruptible. We need to learn to persevere.

Perseverance is choosing to walk in the Spirit or staying submissive to Christ Jesus when pressure is coming from within, or outside ourselves, or both at the same time, to not trust the Lord in the situation. Or to become impatient with God and do it our way.

Suffering and trials are not necessarily the big stuff throwing a spanner in the works. It's the ongoing battle we have with ourselves every day. We persevere so we do not lose sight of God in all situations, major or minor.

Persevering means we're aware this journey isn't always going to be easy. We're willing to hang in there with Christ anyway. This journey may take us on roads we never intended to take. We trust our Shepherd.

It's being able to hang in there, not because we're strong, but because He is stronger and can get us through any and every situation we may have to face.

As we persevere, we grow in character.

Persevering means we're not operating in our own capacity independent of God, it's journeying with Him. And as we journey with Him, we're being moulded into the character of Christ Jesus.

This is why Paul and James can eagerly talk with joy and gladness, because they knew the goal of suffering and tribulations. When the character of Christ becomes more instilled in us, it makes us more secure and stable.

Remember it isn't us becoming stronger, but Christ within us who is becoming stronger.

> I have been crucified with Christ and I no longer live, but Christ lives in me. The life I live in the body, I live by faith in the Son of God, who loved me and gave himself for me. (Galatians 2:20)

It isn't us trying to be better Christians, it's the Holy Spirit instilling in us the character of Christ so we start to respond the way God responds, rather than the way we or the world would respond.

As we're probably aware, this may or may not be working. Without sounding redundant, sufferings, trials and tribulations give us the opportunity to grow in Christ, it doesn't mean we will always choose this path.

We must understand God really does want us to mature and become complete, and He will provide us with many opportunities for this to happen.

We know why the Bible says, "Consider it pure joy and we glory in our suffering."

CHAPTER 27

United in His Word

> In the beginning was the Word, and the Word was with God, and the Word was God. (John 1:1)

For me, the Bible has been like the ocean. For the first seven years of my Christian walk I found it difficult to open the Bible and read, but I had a great love for it. I couldn't open the Bible and read, but I would listen intently to others.

For the first year, it was like standing on the shore of a vast ocean looking out and knowing how great and wonderful the treasures lay within. I loved listening and reading about those who were discovering these truths.

I went to Bible College (a year-long, mission-based course) which took me to another level. We studied the Bible intensely and I absolutely loved it. I still couldn't open the Bible and read.

This time it felt like I had boarded a boat and was looking down into the ocean. I was seeing many things and knew it went to much greater depths.

It was only when I abandoned my excuses and pursued Christ with a sincere, spirit-driven determination the Bible became the true treasure it is to me.

I opened the Bible up at Matthew and the Holy Spirit has consistently illuminated the Scriptures ever since. It's like putting on a deep-sea diving suit and experiencing the true wonders of the ocean.

Let us put on the deep-sea diving suit to go and discover.

When you think about it, the Bible can only be fully appreciated by Five Talent Servants. This is because One Talent Servants or those who have not believed and obeyed Christ, can never understand the Bible, it can only be understood through the Holy Spirit.

The Bible becomes a dangerous book in the hands of man, or it's misinterpreted, leading to grave errors.

The Two Talent Servants fare a little better. They still find themselves in a frustrating position. Because these servants are allowing compromise into their lives, the Bible becomes less applicable.

Some passages can't be applied and many go over their heads. The passages calling for higher living seem out of their grasp.

Two Talent Servants hearts are not fully engaged, and the Bible speaks specifically to hearts which are engaged.

The Bible continually addresses these Two Talent Servants and encourages them to take a hold of Christ and let go of all that entangles them. Because God recognises the ongoing struggle His children have with the flesh and the Spirit, many passages are written to counter this struggle.

The Five Talent Servant is Spirit-led, which in turn yearns and hungers after the Word of God. It's like food, and even unpalatable passages become a necessary addition to the diet.

Because of the willing heart, the call to obedience becomes attainable.

The Word is more than mere words, they are life, truth and direction. Scripture becomes clear and understandable, simple to apply. What was near impossible, is now possible. The Truth is lodged deep within, trust grows and faith blossoms.

Some Christians say one day the Bible was flat, a collection of words and ideas, and when they received Christ the anointing in the Holy Spirit brought the words to life, as though they came off the page and spoke directly into their spirit.

The Bible is a continual source of praise, thanksgiving, worship, security, acceptance, love, truth, hope, discipline, joy, discovery, peace, overcoming, and much more. The servant whose heart is surrendered is engaged with God's Word.

When the Bible speaks of the promises for those who believe and obey, this is a reality, not a hopeful goal. It's a joy to be walking obediently before a loving God and seeing the Word come alive and have it applied to your life.

The sad fact concerning false religions or even trying to please God in our own strength, is true contentment, peace, acceptance, security and other fundamental characteristics of God always seem beyond our reach. We're never able to attain them.

When we're truly walking with Christ, these promises we discover in the Bible are applicable for us. The Bible is speaking directly to us and we accept and experience the truth.

One of the greatest joys in reading the Word is when the Holy Spirit illuminates the Truth. And this happens more often than we realise. As we read Scripture, an understanding of the truth lodges into our hearts, through the Holy Spirit. We notice themes, words, verses, chapters, characters and much more confirming the truths of Christ.

We're being tutored by the Spirit. The Bible is God's 'Word' and God understands it. We need God to always be involved, whether we're reading or listening to others interpret Scripture.

The more you are familiar with God's Truth, the easier it is to discern false teachings.

Any Bible that does not alter the Truth, the Gospel, the Deity of Jesus or the message portrayed through the original texts, is good to read. I'm aware of the controversies surrounding versions of the Bible, especially new versions.

If the Holy Spirit is revealing Christ through these versions, we need to be careful what we demonise. God never intended His Word to be written in one language, or one version.

The original Bible is written in Hebrew, Aramaic and Greek. And in Jesus' day, the Septuagint was the common Bible read which was not Hebrew, but Greek. The Father, Son and Spirit have invested heavily in Their Word and are capable of protecting it from corruption.

There is no perfect English version. God has successfully revealed His Truth throughout the ages up to the present, through many versions aiming to translate and transcribe God's Word honestly.

Psalm 119 is the longest chapter in the Bible and it teaches the benefits of knowing and obeying God's Word.

Psalm 119 is a complete message. If you know of genuine people of God who are struggling, suggest they read Psalm 119 aloud every day for a month. It takes more than 20 minutes, and it's a bath in the essential Bible message.

In the first five verses we see the results of application, deep desire, righteous requirement and personal accountability.

> Blessed are those whose ways are blameless, who walk according to the law of the LORD.
> Blessed are those who keep his statutes and seek him with all their heart – they do no wrong they follow his ways. You have laid down precepts that are to be fully obeyed. Oh, that my ways were steadfast in obeying your decrees. (Psalm 119:1-5)

This is a good summary of what God's Word does, and a cry for His Righteousness we can't find in our own strength.

Chapter 28

United in Obedience

If we have made the Lord Jesus Christ Lord over our lives, obedience is without question.

For us to call Jesus Christ, Lord, that is what He must be. It's a requirement for servants of God.

But sometimes obedience can stir within us unnecessary fears, because we can think of extreme cases for Christians and understand how difficult it must be.

Even though obedience has accomplished such feats as the ark, parting of the Red Sea, the crumbling of the walls of Jericho, walking on water, becoming a missionary in some remote out of the way, foreign land and much more, it's only a small part of obedience.

Obedience is found in many aspects of our lives and is simple. Obedience is knowing good from evil.

> Anyone who lives on milk, being still an infant, is not acquainted with the teaching about righteousness. But solid food is for the mature, who by constant use have trained themselves to distinguish good from evil. (Hebrews 5:13-14)

Here we see a simple concept of obedience, one which we're all capable of. There are obvious evils we know not to entangle ourselves with and when we choose to surrender to the Spirit rather than the sin, we are walking in obedience.

To surrender to Christ when being tempted is the path to maturity. And as we journey on this path, the Holy Spirit makes us aware of how God thinks as opposed to what we previously understood.

It's being obedient by not giving in to sin and being consistent. As that character is maturing within us, the Holy Spirit will reveal areas that we're not aware of and bring our thinking into line with God's way.

Romans 12:1-2 is fully applicable.

> Therefore, I urge you, brothers and sisters, in view of God's mercy, to offer your bodies as a living sacrifice, holy and pleasing to God – this is your true and proper worship.
>
> Do not conform to the pattern of this world, but be transformed by the renewing of your mind. You will be able to test and approve what God's will is – his good, pleasing and perfect will.

Obedience is having your house built on rock and becoming unshakable when the storms come.

> Therefore everyone who hears these words of mine and puts them into practice is like a wise man who built his house on the rock. The rain came down, the streams rose, and the winds blew and beat against that house; yet it did not fall, because it had its foundation on the rock. (Matthew 7:24-25)

This obedience is knowing the ways of Christ (which involves time in His Word and time in His Presence). And it's becoming sensitive to the promptings of the Holy Spirit.

Knowing what Christ requires of us on a daily basis seems simple, but there will be a fight within and outside us.

He said to them all: 'Whoever wants to be my disciple must deny themselves and take up their cross daily and follow me. For whoever wants to save their life will lose it, but whoever loses their life for me will save it.' (Luke 9:23-24)

This is going beyond, not giving into the obvious sins, this is submitting all aspects of our day into the Lord's hand. This is responding the way the Holy Spirit wants us to respond. When we're willing to operate this way, we soon realise how much we're still in control of our thoughts and actions.

Submitting to the teachings of Christ is a duel requiring us to put to death that which isn't of Him.

Trust in the LORD with all your heart and lean not on your own understanding; in all your ways submit to him, and he will make your paths straight. Do not be wise in your own eyes; fear the LORD and shun evil. (Proverbs 3:5-7)

This is a house built on Rock.

Obedience is putting our faith into action. Hebrews 11 is a great chapter on faith and as we look closely at these examples, all of them require action. It's one thing to have faith, but if we do not put it into action, it's useless.

James writes in his second chapter about how faith and action go hand in hand. He tells all Christians that faith without action is useless.

As the body without the spirit is dead, faith without deeds is dead. (James 2:26)

Putting our faith into action doesn't necessarily mean having to do the extraordinary, like some of the seemingly impossible accomplishments found in the Bible. It's obediently walking in what we have learnt from Christ.

> But whoever looks intently into the perfect law giving freedom, and continues in it – not forgetting what they have heard, but doing it – they will be blessed in what they do. (James 1:25)

Obedience is more than accomplishing the extraordinary, it's obediently walking in the ordinary.

It means we're reacting and responding the way God's Word teaches us. We're sensitive to the promptings of the Holy Spirit, when to reach out practically and when we're submissive to Christ when the pressures from outside us and within try to influence us away from our Lord.

Chapter 29

Biblical Examples

The Bible is full of great examples of Five Talent Servants, and as we look at some, we see how we can have the same attitude.

Starting with Abel, we see a sacrificial life. Abel brought before God the best of his herd with a grateful and God-fearing heart (Genesis 4:2-4).

A sacrificial life isn't merely bringing our tithes and offerings, it's our whole life.

> Therefore, I urge you, brothers and sisters, in view of God's mercy, to offer your bodies as a living sacrifice, holy and pleasing to God – this is your true and proper worship. (Romans 12:1)

Lay before God, everything. Living a sacrificial life is allowing God into every part of our lives, allowing His will and His way to lead us.

Enoch walked with God (Genesis 5:24). When we faithfully walk with Christ in all aspects of our life, this pleases God. Being mindful of Him no matter where we find ourselves, is a safeguard that includes the Holy Spirit in all areas of our life.

Noah faithfully built the ark God instructed him to build. Noah put his faith into action, following the instructions of the Lord.

Putting our faith into action includes both providential and specific callings.

Providential is what we're already doing on a daily basis in our home life, workplace, church life, social life. Being faithful in these areas is putting our faith into action.

It's being obedient to what we know in our hearts God is specifically calling us to do, from the simplest of acts to great feats. Being obedient to what we know Christ requires, is putting our faith into action. Faith and action go hand in hand.

Abraham believed in God despite the seemingly impossible tasks ahead of him. Abraham trusted God. Trusting God is an important foundation bringing stability in all circumstances.

> And we know in all things God works for the good of those who love him, who have been called according to his purpose. (Romans 8:28)

Knowing God is present in all things we face, gives us the assurance we're not alone and if we allow Him, He will give us the ability to remain tender-hearted and sure-footed through the most trying of times.

Joseph trusted God's promise ahead of him. Joseph was able to faithfully endure unfair treatment because he trusted His God was testing and preparing him. God's promise was always before him, giving him the ability to stay obedient to God and those who had authority over him, despite ill treatment and false accusations.

Having earthly missions is good, but our heavenly destination is our ultimate reward. When we truly know where we're going, this encourages us to endure and persevere, holding fast to the promise ahead of us.

Praise be to the God and Father of our Lord Jesus Christ. In his great mercy he has given us new birth into a living hope through the resurrection of Jesus Christ from the dead, and into an inheritance that can never perish, spoil or fade.

This inheritance is kept in heaven for you, who through faith are shielded by God's power until the coming of the salvation that is ready to be revealed in the last time. In all this you greatly rejoice, though for a little while you may have had to suffer grief in all kinds of trials. (1 Peter 1:3-6)

Knowing where we're eventually going to end up gives us great hope and the ability to endure without giving up.

I consider that our present sufferings are not worth comparing with the glory that will be revealed in us. (Romans 8:18)

Moses was willing to give up worldly privilege and prestige for the sake of Christ.

By faith Moses, when he had grown up, refused to be known as the son of Pharaoh's daughter.

He chose to be mistreated along with the people of God rather than enjoy the fleeting pleasures of sin. He regarded disgrace for the sake of Christ as of greater value than the treasures of Egypt, because he was looking ahead to his reward. (Hebrews 11:24-26)

Moses wanted to be where God wanted him. We may not have to face a similar choice, however, having a desire to be where God wants us will always lead us toward Him and not away from Him.

Knowing we're in Christ's will, rather than the will of ourselves or others is an important place to be. To pursue the will of Christ over and above anything this world may entice you away with is the highest road you can travel.

If your desire is to be where God wants you, and you have let Him know this, trust He has heard you and is big enough to take care of the rest.

Being in His will may not be obvious if we're looking for the spectacular. God carefully crafted my path so I would end up in a processing factory, and His Grace has kept me there.

God can work anywhere He chooses. Find God in the present, don't wait only for the future, or get stuck in nostalgic past, experiencing Christ now is the utmost importance.

Joshua trusted God's Word and promise rather than give in to the fear of the enemy awaiting them in Canaan. Despite what he saw he fully trusted his God was more than capable of helping them.

When all of Israel fell into despair and fear, Joshua cried out to the people.

> Only do not rebel against the LORD. And do not be afraid of the people of the land, because we will devour them. Their protection is gone, but the LORD is with us. Do not be afraid of them. (Numbers 14:9)

In this life, Satan and his minions will use many tactics to discourage us on this journey. Whether they are subtle hindrances entangling our feet, up to a full-frontal attack of threats and intimidation, even manifestations of demons and pure evil, our trust remains anchored in our Lord and Saviour, Jesus Christ.

These spirits and forces have no authority over us. We have authority over them solely through the power and favour of the Lord Jesus Christ our Saviour.

Gideon, despite his weakness and witnessing continual defeat within his land (Judges 6:1-6, 11-15), chose to trust in God's strength. Once he was convinced God truly was on his side, he went fearlessly into battle with only three hundred soldiers against one hundred and thirty five thousand swordsman (Judges 8:10).

Trusting God beyond our experience and history is a path God may lead us on, and knowing God is involved is the real key.

David gives us many examples of a Five Talent Servant despite his shortcomings, who became the greatest king Israel has known. In the Gospels, Jesus is referred to as, 'the son of David' (Matthew 20:30-31, 21:9,15).

Despite manifest failings at various times, David trusts his God for protection against powerful enemies and beasts (1 Samuel 17:34-37). David successfully defeated a lion, a bear and the giant, Goliath.

We need not fear what foe confronts us, even if the foe is death. If you are in God's hands, no matter what the outcome, it will be victorious.

David feared God over choosing to bring a quick end to a major problem. King Saul relentlessly pursued David to kill him, but there were a couple of perfect opportunities for David to kill Saul.

> The men said, 'This is the day the LORD spoke of when he said to you, "I will give your enemy into your hands for you to deal with as you wish."' (1 Samuel 24:4-7)

David crept up unnoticed and cut off a corner of Saul's robe. Afterward, David was conscience-stricken for having cut off a corner of his robe. He said to his men,

> 'The LORD forbid I should do such a thing to my master, the LORD's anointed, or lay my hand on him; for he is the anointed of the LORD.' With these words David sharply rebuked his men and did not allow them to attack Saul.

David had another opportunity to kill Saul, but he didn't (1 Samuel 26:7-12).

Five Talent Servants trust God in trials and tribulations, no matter how dark the situation may become, their strength and peace rest in Christ. They don't end the problem in their own strength or ability, without the Will of God.

This calls for great trust, wisdom and maturity.

Faced with an urgent matter needing an immediate response, David didn't rush into it without first consulting God. When David sought refuge under the king of Philistine, Achish, the king looked upon him with favour and even trusted David enough to ask him to join him in battle against Saul and the Israelites.

Obviously, the other Philistine commanders didn't think this wise, and David and his men were turned back on their journey (1 Samuel 29:1-11).

When David and his men arrived back at Ziklag, their place of refuge, the Amalekites had attacked and carried off everyone there.

> David and his men reached Ziklag, they found it destroyed by fire and their wives and sons and daughters taken captive. David and his men wept aloud until they had no strength left to weep. (1 Samuel 30:3-4)

The men wanted to stone David to death, but David found strength in the Lord. David consulted God and asked if he would successfully pursue the Amalekites and be victorious, 'Yes', was God's answer.

> Do not be anxious about anything, but in every situation, by prayer and petition, with thanksgiving, present your requests to God. (Philippians 4:6)

We can in all situations, even urgent ones, have God involved.

When King David bought the Ark of the Covenant back, he danced and worshipped before the Lord with all his might and without inhibitions (2 Samuel 6:12-15).

David was a worshipper of God and Psalms gives us an insight into David's heart toward his Creator.

Being a worshipper of God is more than song and dance, it involves our whole lives.

> Therefore, I urge you, brothers and sisters, in view of God's mercy, to offer your bodies as a living sacrifice, holy and pleasing to God – this is your true and proper worship. (Romans 12:1)

Worshipping Christ from our hearts is where true worship springs from.

King David subdued all surrounding enemies, the Lord gave David victory wherever he went.

As Christians, we're in a battle, and we're at war. We're at war on three fronts. Our fleshy, carnal nature (Romans 8:12-13), the pattern of this world (Romans 12:2) and the spiritual realm (Ephesians 6:10-18). That should keep us on our toes, or on our knees, for the rest of our lives.

Ruth humbly served her mother-in-law and Boaz (the book of Ruth). Ruth's humble attitude and her willingness to be a lowly servant for the benefit of others is acknowledged by God.

Ruth became the great grandmother of King David and is included in the genealogy of the Messiah (Matthew 1:5).

Humility is important to God and Jesus gives us a great example in John 13:3-5,

> Jesus knew that the Father had put all things under his power,

> and that he had come from God and was returning to God; so he got up from the meal, took off his outer clothing, and wrapped a towel around his waist.
>
> After that, he poured water into a basin and began to wash his disciples' feet, drying them with the towel that was wrapped around him.

Jesus explains what He has done.

> When he had finished washing their feet, he put on his clothes and returned to his place. 'Do you understand what I have done for you?' he asked them.
>
> 'You call me "Teacher" and "Lord," and rightly so, for that is what I am. Now that I, your Lord and Teacher, have washed your feet, you should wash one another's feet. I have set you an example that you should do as I have done for you.
>
> 'Truly I tell you, no servant is greater than his master, nor is a messenger greater than the one who sent him. Now that you know these things, you will be blessed if you do them.' (John 13:12-17)

Humility and having the attitude of a servant is highly esteemed by Christ, when it's done in the Spirit of the Lord.

King Hezekiah cleans out the Temple of God and reinstitutes the role of the Levites and priests (2 Chronicles 29).

> Don't you know that you yourselves are God's temple and that God's Spirit dwells in your midst? (1 Corinthians 3:16)

Keeping our Temple clean is important.

Five Talent Servants are brave enough to pray,

> Search me, God, and know my heart; test me and know my anxious thoughts. See if there is any offensive way in me, and lead me in the way everlasting. (Psalm 139:23-24)

King Josiah purges his land of idols and structures used for the worship of idols. As we're to keep our Temple clean, we're to purge any outside influences making us unclean.

Even though we have influence in the world around us, we're not to let the world have influence in us.

> Do not be yoked together with unbelievers. For what do righteousness and wickedness have in common? What harmony is there between Christ and Belial? Or what does a believer have in common with an unbeliever? What agreement is there between the temple of God and idols? For we're the temple of the living God.
>
> As God has said: 'I will live with them and walk among them, and I will be their God, and they will be my people.'
>
> 'Come out from them and be separate, says the Lord. Touch no unclean thing, and I will receive you.' And, 'I will be a Father to you, and you will be my sons and daughters, says the Lord Almighty.' (2 Corinthians 6:14-18)

This is by no means telling us to separate ourselves completely, like monks in a monastery. It's telling us not to get ourselves involved in things leading us to sin. We need to be careful how we interact with and react to people around us.

In the book of Ezra, we see the reconstruction of God's Temple in Jerusalem. First under the guidance of Zerubbabel, governor of Judah and Joshua the High Priest, they build an altar, and the foundations of the Temple (Ezra 3:1-10). Over time, the Temple is built and Ezra comes back to Jerusalem from exile to encourage the Israelites to stay pure and dedicated to God (Ezra 7).

Without question, the Father, Son and the Holy Spirit must be the foundation and cornerstone of our lives.

Nehemiah is anguished over the ruin of Jerusalem's wall and gates.

> They said to me, 'Those who survived the exile and are back in the province are in great trouble and disgrace. The wall of Jerusalem is broken down, and its gates have been burned with fire.' When I heard these things, I sat down and wept. For some days I mourned and fasted and prayed before the God of heaven. (Nehemiah 1:3-4)

The walls surrounding the city were an important defence, and the gates were important to regulate who could leave and, crucially, who could enter.

What made Jerusalem even more valuable, was this was the city God chose to dwell in. For the Sacred city of Jerusalem to be defenceless against the raids of the enemy was especially devastating.

Our defensive walls surrounding our lives are important to God, these defensive walls stop the tactics of the enemy, within and outside us, and stop sin entering our lives.

Five Talent Servants are always checking our walls and gates, and where there is a breach – pride, lust, unbelief, grumbling – we're to repair and stay vigilant.

Asking God to show us weaknesses in our defences may be a scary prospect, but if we truly want God's best in our lives, it's a sacrifice we will be willing to endure.

These are a few examples from the Old Testament. There are many more, including the New Testament (Peter, John, Philip,

Steven, Paul and more). We can find many examples of Five Talent Servants in and outside the Bible.

The Bible continually gives us examples of what it is to be a Five Talent Servant. When we open our spiritual eyes to this, we will start to see it everywhere in Scripture.

Chapter 30

Conclusion

God's intention for our lives is to be Five Talent Servants.

The parable of the five talents and the parable of the ten minas have traditionally been interpreted as being about our talents and abilities, and whether we're using them to bring glory to God.

These parables refer to three types of people, the non-Christian, the Christian who is still compromising and the Christian who has surrendered with all their heart.

The One Talent Servant has rejected the promptings and encounters of the Holy Spirit. God hasn't hidden Himself from mankind, but mankind has blinded themselves to Him. Romans 1:18-31 says how foolish mankind has become because of their rejection of the Truth.

All, however, will be accountable.

> It is written: 'As surely as I live,' says the Lord, 'every knee will bow before me; every tongue will acknowledge God.'
> Each of us will give an account of ourselves to God. (Romans 14:11-12)

The Two Talent Servant has obeyed the Holy Spirit by making Jesus Christ their Lord, but still continues to allow their fleshy carnal nature to have its way.

> For the flesh desires what is contrary to the Spirit, and the Spirit what is contrary to the flesh. They are in conflict with each other, so you are not to do whatever you want. (Galatians 5:17)

Our carnal nature is always wanting to live and lead. If we don't recognise this, whether it's subtle and deceitful, or blatantly rebelling, we remain Two Talent Servants until we submit to Christ and die to its influence.

The Five Talent Servant is what the Bible is always pointing us toward.

> But whatever were gains to me I consider loss for the sake of Christ. What is more, I consider everything a loss because of the surpassing worth of knowing Christ Jesus my Lord, for whose sake I have lost all things. I consider them garbage that I may gain Christ. (Philippians 3:7-8)

To know Christ this way means we have stopped striving in the flesh and Christ is being included in all facets of our lives.

The only obstacle preventing us being Five Talent Servants, is ourselves.

There is no foe within or outside ourselves that can stop the Holy Spirit enabling us to do what is right. There is no darkness the Light of Christ can't penetrate. There is no catastrophe too overwhelming for God. There is no problem Wisdom can't navigate.

There is no sin making it past the Cross of Christ.

God's availability is inexhaustible. Christ's tower of refuge is impenetrable. Every part of Christ's armour is true and proven. The Holy Spirit intercedes on our behalf before God concerning His will in our lives (Romans 8:26-27).

Jesus is at God's right hand, interceding for us (Romans 8:34).

Because we love Him, He works all things for the good. If God is for us, who can be against us (Romans 8:31)?

From Genesis through to Revelation, God has made Himself known and has revealed how we're to respond to Him. His desire for us has always been that we become 'Five Talent Servants'.

Every person aspiring to be the best they can in the Spirit of Truth always has the simple first step.

Ask for your Father's help.

*Thanks for reading this book.
If you would like to get in contact,
please email:*
jason.selinagroube@outlook.com

www.ingramcontent.com/pod-product-compliance
Lightning Source LLC
Chambersburg PA
CBHW051437290426
44109CB00016B/1589